teens ask. teens answer.

Questions and answers from "What's on Your Mind?"— a column in <u>Scholastic Scope</u>, popular classroom magazine for teenagers.

selected and edited by
FRAN CLARO

SCHOLASTIC BOOK SERVICES
New York Toronto London Auckland Sydney Tokyo

Copyright © 1978 by Scholastic Magazines, Inc. All rights reserved. Published by Scholastic Book Services, a division of Scholastic Magazines, Inc.

12 11 10 9 8 7 6 5 4 3 2 1   1   8 9/7 0 1 2 3/8

CONTENTS

Dear Reader:

What's on your mind? Are you arguing with your parents? Do you have trouble making friends? Or are you worried about how to get along with your steady?

Do you sometimes feel you're the only one in your crowd who needs advice? That it would be terrific if someone said, "I know just how you feel because the same thing happened to me"?

Scope magazine receives many letters from readers like you asking for advice about things that are troubling them. Who gives this advice? Other *Scope* readers, because they have the answers you are all looking for.

TEENS ASK. TEENS ANSWER. is made up of letters sent to *Scope* and the replies that come from young people all over the country. Often there is more than one solution. And sometimes the solutions differ because there is never just one way to face a problem.

Maybe you have some of the problems dealt with in this book. We hope the advice given will help you face them in a new way.

Fran Claro
Associate Editor
Scholastic Scope

I

FAMILY:

Parents

Question

Many times when I try to talk to my parents, they ignore me. When they do listen, they don't seem to understand what I'm saying. I've tried talking to my older sisters, but they act just like my parents. What should I do?

C.M., Sacramento, CA

Answers

1. Tell your parents that they are ignoring you. They may not realize it. Explain to them that you want to tell them about things that bother you. Explain that you can't tell them your problems if they won't listen.

R.H., Gainesville, TX

2. Ask your guidance counselor for help with your parents. Maybe she/he could meet with your parents and discuss your problem with them. If this doesn't work, write a letter to them. That should help them understand your feelings.

M.A., Fort Lewis, WA

Question

My mother expects too much of me. She thinks I should be really smart in school — because she was. But I'm not as smart as she thinks I am. How can I tell her this? I don't want her to be too disappointed in me.

R.C., Bronx, NY

Answers

1. I have the same problem, and I know how you feel. Ask your mother to help you with your homework. Tell her you do your best. You are different people. You have different minds. Why not put your minds together? You could both learn new things.

G.C., San Diego, CA

2. When you're about to have a test, tell your mom. Then study hard. Do it where she'll notice it. Then she'll know you tried your best.

W.R.S., Pelahatchie, MS

3. I don't think a mother should expect so

2

much from her child. A child should not be pushed to be smart. You should tell your mother that it's your life, not hers.

L.A., So. Pasadena, CA

Question

My problem is with my mother. Every boy I go out with, she compares with my old boyfriend. She won't let me go out with anyone more than once. All she ever talks about is my old boyfriend. But I'm in love with someone else. How can I make her understand?

D.D.L., Coden, AL

Answer

Explain your feelings to your mother. Tell her you are not a little girl any more. You must go through life picking your own friends. I feel it is wrong to judge a person by another person.

F.B., Richmond Hill, NY

Question

I am having a very hard time at home. It seems that the more I do, the more my parents expect of me. Whatever I say, we always end up fighting. They seem to think that just because they buy me things, this means they love me.

L.G., Dover, NJ

Answers

1. Try to get a job. Then you won't be around your parents so much. You won't argue so much. And, if you had a job, you could buy things for yourself.

L.R., Galesburg, IL

2. All parents have different ways of showing their love. Try to understand your parents' point of view.

T.H., Eaton Rapids, MI

Question

My parents are divorced. I am now living with my father. I am having problems that girls my age have. My dad doesn't seem to understand. I can't go to my mother. She has remarried. She doesn't want her new children and husband to know about me. What should I do?

B.D.M.

Answers

1. I think you should talk to one of your girlfriends' mothers. Or talk to a teacher you are close to. I'm sure you can find someone who will listen to your problems.

L.J., Davenport, FL

2. Talk to one of your girlfriends' older

sisters. Or read some books that give advice about problems. Or talk to a teacher or a guidance counselor. Someone will be able to help you.

C.M., Oyster Bay, NY

3. You should go to your mother. You say that she doesn't want anything to do with you. But that is wrong. She is still your mother.

S.G., Chicago, IL

Question

I have a problem with my parents. They don't trust me to go out with my boyfriend. They like my boyfriend, and I don't get into trouble much. What can I do?

B.L., Alexandria Bay, NY

Answers

1. If I were you, I'd ask your parents why they won't let you date your boyfriend. I'd also tell them that you're not a baby any more. Maybe they will understand and let you go out.

L.M., Red Creek, NY

2. Talk to your parents. Tell them how you feel. Say that they probably got to go out a little when they were young. Ask them to give you a chance.

B.C., Slinger, WI

3. Don't feel bad. My parents won't let me go to a movie by myself. They think I'm going to meet my boyfriend there. But there are ways of seeing your boyfriend without going out on planned dates. For example, if you go to home football games, maybe you'll see him there.

K.M., Stow, OH

4. I think you should sit down with your parents. Try to discuss the problem with them. Then call up your boyfriend, or invite him over. And let him talk to them. Maybe they've got a reason to be worried. If you give in a little, maybe they will, too. Try to compromise with them.

B.J.W., Campobello, SC

Question

My parents and I don't get along. I am the oldest and only girl in the family. I have three brothers. And we are always fighting. I don't know whether it's me or what I'm doing. Can anybody help me?

Need Help, WI

Answers

1. First, maybe you don't talk to your parents enough. Second, it's not unusual for your brothers to fight with you. I have three sisters and a brother. They are all on my back. Try to ignore your brothers when they start fighting.

2. I'm the only girl in my family, too. I also have three brothers. We fight a lot. So don't worry. It's not just you. I think everyone fights with brothers and sisters now and then.

S.A.L., Sparta, TN

3. It's not only you. Since you're the oldest, your parents may figure you're responsible. When there's fighting, try to reason with your brothers.

D.M.L., Roselle, IL

Question

I have been driving for about two years. But my parents don't trust me with the family car. How can I convince them that I am a careful person?

J.B., Pelahatchie, MS

Answers

1. Show your parents that you are a responsible person. Be extra careful when you drive in the car with them. Use the car to go on errands for them. If they still don't trust you, get a job. Save your money and buy your own car.

B.G., Indianapolis, IN

7

2. Take your parents for a test drive. Let them pick the route to take. Tell them not to talk to you when you are driving. Prove to them that you are careful.

T.A., Tucson, AZ

Question

Last summer, while I was on vacation, I was questioned by narcotics agents. I told my mother about this, and she was very understanding for a while.

Now, for some reason, she doesn't trust me. I am not allowed to stay out late or go to parties. How can I get my mother to trust me again?

N.W.

Answer

Maybe your mother has forgotten about the drug question. You may be doing something else that is upsetting her. Ask her why she has stopped trusting you. Talk it over with your father, too. You may find out what's really bothering your mother.

L.M., East Peoria, IL

Question

I have just finished an interest survey. I scored high in computational interests. This suggests that I should become a secretary.

My father wants me to be a secretary. But I want to be an auctioneer. But I scored only average in being persuasive. How can I get my father to let me be an auctioneer? Do you think those tests are really so important?

J.H., Excelsior Springs, MO

Answers

1. I don't think your father will be angry if you decide to become an auctioneer. Just hang in there. It's your life. Do what you think is best.

L.W., Arnold, CA

2. If you really want to be an auctioneer, then stick to it. If you're not interested in becoming a secretary, you probably shouldn't become one. It might make you very unhappy. Explain to your father how you feel. I don't think that tests can always tell everything about a person.

D.G. Manassas, VA

3. Don't pay any attention to those tests. I rated high in mechanics in a test. And I wouldn't know the first thing about it. Try to tell your father, in a nice way, that you have to live your own life.

P.J., Rock Falls, IL

Question

I'll soon have a driver's license. I've saved

money for a long time to buy a new car. But my parents want me to get a used car. They think I don't have enough driving experience to handle a new car. I think that since *I* saved the money, I should buy what I want. What do other people think? Should I buy a new or used car?

C.D., Passaic, NJ

Answers

1. Don't buy a used car. It will only cause you a lot of trouble. Fixing up a used car costs money. By the time you get it running well, you will have spent as much as a new car costs.

L.C., Ethridge, TN

2. Buy a used car. Prove to your parents that you can handle it and keep it in good condition. Once your parents trust you, trade it in and get a new car.

J.H., Middletown, NJ

3. Whether the car is new or used isn't really important. What is important is how well the car runs. Have a talk with your parents, and tell them this. Then buy a good car at a price you can afford.

R.R., Williamsburg, VA

Question

I like to cook, but my mother doesn't want

me to use the kitchen. She doesn't think I'm responsible enough. What can I do?

H.H., Pleasantville, NY

Answers

1. Ask your mother to stay in the kitchen and watch you prepare a meal. When you have finished cooking *and* cleaning up, ask her opinion. If you have followed the recipe carefully and left the kitchen as neat as you found it, she will probably change her mind. If this doesn't work, you might take a home economics course in cooking.

D.E., Buena, NJ

2. With your mother's permission, start off by cooking something simple. Follow the recipe carefully. Clean up the kitchen when you are finished. When your mother sees how neat and careful you are, she'll probably let you cook fancier foods.

C.L., Merced, CA

Question

I go to a boys' boarding school. My parents sent me here last year and again this year. I don't like it here at all. What should I do?

R.W.E., Mexico, MO

Answers

1. Talk it over with your parents. Tell them

you don't like this school. Maybe you could find out about some schools you'd like to go to. Get your parents' opinions about the other schools. They may agree with you. If they don't change their minds, stay at this school. But keep writing to your parents about why you dislike it.

S.L., Albany, CA

2. Tell your parents how you feel about this school. Tell them the one or two things that bother you the most about the school. They may see that you are complaining about real problems. Good luck.

S.C., Salem, MA

Question

We are twin sisters whose parents are divorced. We live with our father. He has a lot of money and buys us anything we want. But he won't let us visit our mother much because he thinks she is a "bad influence." How can we convince him that we love her and want to see her?

"Troubled Two"

Answers

1. Remind your father that he loved your mother once. At one time he wanted to spend a lot of time with her. Tell him that you *still* love her and want to spend some time with her.

T.C., Vernon, NY

2. Ask your father to let you visit your mother to find out if she has changed. Tell him that after visiting her, you may agree with what he says. Or you may find out that she is not a bad influence. Tell your father that just because he doesn't get along with her doesn't mean that you can't still love her.

A.L.A., Williamsburg, VA

Question

I'm 16, and my parents won't let me have a boyfriend. But I've been going out with someone secretly for six months. When my parents found out, they told me to stop seeing him or leave home. I really love this guy. I don't want to stop seeing him. We have cut school to be together. If my parents find out about this, they will kick me out. So I don't plan to do this again. How can I convince my parents that I'm old enough to go out with him?

D.F., Chicago, IL

Answers

1. It's too late. You've already spoiled it by seeing him secretly. But you might talk to your parents and ask them why they won't let you have a boyfriend.

J.R., Streamwood, IL

2. Talk to your parents. Tell them they are

being unreasonable. My parents were very strict with my older sister. When she went to college and lived on campus, she really went wild. She would stay out very late at night. My parents are a lot easier on me. Be patient with your parents and don't lose your temper. You might be *in* love with this guy, but I doubt that you love him. I thought this way about my first boyfriend, too. There will be others.

T.M., Paragould, AR

3. When I first met a guy I wanted to go out with, my parents didn't want me to see him. I'm lucky because I have an older sister. My boyfriend and I started doubling with my sister and her boyfriend. Gradually, my parents let us go out alone. Ask your parents if you can double. My mother feels there is safety in numbers. Maybe your parents feel the same way.

"A Friend," Plymouth, IL

Question

My mother is always after me to clean my room and clear off my desk. I like to keep my desk the way it is. It's my room. I feel I should be able to do what I want with it. Does anyone know a way around this problem?

S.S., Elnora, NY

Answers

1. I've never been able to keep my room clean until now. My cousin was coming to visit, so I had to clean up the mess. I did it slowly. First day, got rid of unneeded clothes. Second day, books. Third day, settled back in, organizing things. Fourth day, changed the furniture around and made it look nice. Now I feel great. Everything has its place.

N.B., Merrick, NY

2. Tell your mom that this is where you sleep. It is your room. Tell her you'll clean it when you're ready to do it.

J.H., Galesburg, IL

3. I had the same problem. Finally, my mother just gave up. One day, I realized what a mess it was. It looked like a junkyard. So I found a box and put everything into it. Then I fixed up my room. Now I do this every two months. It really scores points with my mom.

T.B., Bellevue, MI

Question

My mother got a job. Now she seems to be so busy with her work that she doesn't have any time for me, my sister, and my brother. How can we get her to see that we need more of her time?

"A Friend in Need"

Answers

1. Help out with things around the house. For instance, you could do the grocery shopping, or cleaning. That will probably give her more free time. Then you can suggest things that the whole family can do together.

N.B., Minnetonka, MN

2. Tell her that you, and your brother and sister, need more of her time. If she doesn't listen, prove it to her. You might ask her to help one of you with homework. When she sees how much you need her, she'll probably get the message.

E.B., Thomasville, GA

3. You're probably used to getting a lot of attention from your mother. Now you miss it. Many mothers work *and* take good care of their families. As time goes by, you'll learn to be more independent and you'll be better off.

D.K., Miami, FL

Question

I lived in a foster home for nine years. Now I am living with my mother. She has 11 children. Five of us are living with her now. The rest of the children will join us later. I get along pretty well with my mother. But if she asks me to do something and I make a mistake, she screams at me and fights with me. I've been having very bad headaches because of this. Sometimes I feel like running away. What can I do to get along better with her?

"Unhappy"

Answers

1. Talk to her and tell her how you feel. If this doesn't work, talk to someone you are close to who would understand. That person may be able to help you. If this still isn't the answer, ask someone if you could live with them for awhile, until your mother changes her ways.

P.M., Washington, D.C.

2. Your mother is probably very nervous. After all, she does have a huge family. Give her as much peace and rest as you possibly can. Try to keep the other kids off her back. You have to realize that you are doing this not just for yourself. But you are doing this to help your mother, too.

E.R., Orangeburg, SC

3. Tell your mother that you're getting headaches because she yells at you. Tell her you're trying your best, but she has to be more patient. Explain that if she shows more patience, you might not have head-

aches. And you might stop making so many mistakes.

White Shield, ND

Question

I go to a boys' boarding school, and I only come home on weekends. When I'm home, my parents get angry with me for spending so much time with my girlfriend. What can I do?

V.A.M., Vineland, NJ

Answers

1. Your parents probably feel left out of your life. Try spending Saturday with your girlfriend and Sunday with your parents. You could alternate the days each weekend.

Students, Newport, OR

2. Spend some time with your girlfriend *and* your parents. Invite her to your home. Or invite her to go bowling — or something — with you and your parents. Ask your parents how they feel about this solution. They'll probably be very understanding.

C.H., Saginaw, MI

3. If you lived at home, you would spend a few hours each day with your girlfriend. Explain this to your parents. Tell them that the time you spend with her on weekends is

the same amount you would see her if you lived at home.

T.N., Springfield, MA

Question

My problem is that I live in a very bad part of town. I want to move, but my parents say we can't. I'm very embarrassed to invite friends over. What can I do?

W.J., Monticello, NY

Answers

1. If you can't move, fix the place up. Do it yourself. It won't have to cost much.

W.R., Spartanburg, NC

2. I think you are selfish. Your parents are probably doing all they can to give you a decent place to live.

V.T., Denver, CO

Question

I'm 16, and I've been going out with a 26-year-old man for the past year. My father wants me to stop seeing him. But my mother thinks it's all right to go out with an older man. I don't know what to do.

D.W., Needesha, KS

Answers

1. Don't spend all your time with this older man. Date some guys who are closer to your age.

D.H., Pittsburgh, PA

2. Ask your mother to talk to your father. Maybe they can work out a solution. Then you and this man might discuss the solution with them.

P.A.K., Owensboro, KY

Question

I am very unhappy because I am adopted. I have two sisters and a brother who are also adopted. I guess I love my present parents. At the same time, it hurts me to know that I wasn't wanted when I was born.

Recently, my brother got busted for using drugs. This really upset my parents. I wanted to comfort them. I couldn't, though, because I know they are not my real parents. I guess I should be happy that I'm not in an orphanage any more. But sometimes I feel so unhappy that I want to die. Do most adopted children feel this way?

"Adopted"

Answers

1. Your parents must love you, your brother, and sisters very much because they chose all of you. Any comfort you can give your parents will be appreciated. When I first learned that I was adopted, I felt like dying. Then I realized how much people must really want children, if they adopt them. Now I understand how lucky I am. I try hard to make my parents proud of me.

J.A., Milwaukee, WI

2. I'm adopted. My present parents told me that I shouldn't care about my real parents because they gave me up, and didn't care about the kind of home I would get. I know you might think of your real parents once in a while. But don't worry about them. Now you have parents. You should love them as if they were your real parents.

L.P., WI

3. Why don't you try to find out about your real parents? Tell your present parents how you feel, and maybe they will understand. Tell your brother he should appreciate his parents more. They were loving and kind enough to adopt him.

"Huntington Beach," CA

4. I'm in a similar situation. I live with an aunt and uncle, and I never see my parents. Should having a home with people who love you make you unhappy? Your real parents are only your biological parents. There is another meaning of the word "parent." Parents

are people who look after and care for children. Have you thought about your adoptive parents? They have loved and cared for you, and your sisters, and brother. That means they are parents in one of the true meanings of the word.

K.C., Chicago, IL

5. Why don't you ask your brother and sisters how they feel? Maybe your parents are making things worse by talking about the fact that you are adopted. Your real parents may not have wanted you. But that doesn't mean that your adoptive parents feel the same way. You call them your "present parents." That sounds as if you don't feel very secure. Maybe you can't be blamed for feeling this way. But, I think you should love these parents as much as you would love your real parents.

J.U., Pearl River, NY

6. I'm 15 and adopted. I have two brothers and a sister who are also adopted. My adoptive father died 10 years ago. Maybe we *weren't* wanted by our real parents. But we are lucky that there are people who are willing to take children who are strangers and treat them as their own. These parents deserve a special love. Why don't you give it to them? I only wish my dad could know how much I love him.

"Adopted and Happy"

7. I was adopted. When I was born my mother was very sick. She couldn't keep me because she couldn't care for me. She showed her love by giving me away. I think she had a lot of courage to do this. Maybe you were wanted when you were born, too. Maybe you just couldn't be kept. Comfort your parents when they need someone. And maybe they will comfort you when you need them.

"Also Adopted"

Question

I want to grow my hair longer, but my father makes me cut it. How can I get him to change?

"Short Haired," Alfred, ME

Answers

1. You can't change your father, but you can talk to him. Explain why you want your hair a little longer. Then keep it clean and combed. And cut it before it gets too long.

K.J., St. Paul, MN

2. Tell your father that people wear longer hair these days. Then ask him if he went along with the trends when he was young.

S.M.B., Jennings, MO

Question

My boyfriend used to smoke pot. He

doesn't anymore, but people still talk about him. My mother believes all the stories she hears about him. How can I convince her that he's stopped using pot?

P.H., Republic of Honduras

Answers

1. Ask your boyfriend to tell your mother himself that he has stopped smoking pot. If she hears it from *him*, she might believe it. Remind her that once rumors get started, they are hard to stop.

D.M., Spartansburg, SC

2. Have your boyfriend visit you at home more often. Then your mother will get to know him better, and she may trust him more. Also, tell your boyfriend to try to ignore the rumors about him. If he does this, the rumors will die down.

B.F., Indian Orchard, MA

Question

My father, sister, and brother all work for the local police department. They no longer trust me since two of my friends got busted for shoplifting. How can I prove to them that I'm clean?

K.M.C., CO

Answers

1. Stay away from people who shoplift. Prove to your family that you *are* clean. Remember this saying: "If friends get into trouble when you're with them, you are just as guilty as they are."

J.R., New Orleans, LA

2. Explain to your family that you are not like your friends. Tell your parents that you need their trust. If you need money to go shopping, ask your parents. Pay back the money you borrow from them as soon as you can. They will probably learn to trust you.

K.S., D.H., Gainesville, GA

3. Stop seeing your friends who shoplift for a while. If this doesn't help, try making new friends.

D.W., D.M., Gainesville, GA

Question

Every weekend, Dad starts drinking. Mom is not in the best of health. He is really driving her crazy. I'm so afraid they will break up. Everyone else in the family is married and "out." I'm 15, and Mom says I'm the only reason she puts up with Dad. I don't know what to do.

In-the-Middle, NY

Answers

1. I think you should go and live somewhere else. Let your parents settle this. Then you can go back home. The same thing happened to me. Now I am in a school home. And it's much better.

J.M., Auburn, CA

2. If your parents are staying together for your sake, it isn't fair to them. When you finally leave home, they will probably break up anyway. Talk to them. Tell them how you feel.

V.L., Blacksburg, VA

3. You might be much better off if your parents split up. I was in a similar situation. But my parents got divorced. My dad remarried. Life is a joy now. I also have a mother who cares for me.

D.G., Memphis, TN

4. Have you ever heard of Alateen? It's an organization that helps teenagers whose parents have drinking problems. I know they could help you. They helped me.

B.G., New York, NY

(For more information about Alateen, write to: Alateen, P. O. Box 182, Madison Square Station, New York, NY 10010. Answers come in unmarked envelopes.)

Question

My mother and I are always fighting. Every time we fight, I feel like running away. Could you give me some advice?

L.C., Spencer, MA

Answers

1. I ran away once. My friends talked me into going back home. When I went back, I told my mother that I have feelings, too. She understood. Now we get along pretty well together.

Try talking to your mother about your problems. If this doesn't work, try writing her a letter. Ask your father to help you, too.

C.C., Maywood, IL

2. You and your mother probably fight because you're not honest with each other. Maybe you both try to hide things from each other. Tell your mother you'll always tell her the truth. Then you'll probably get along better.

A.G., Framingham, MA

Brothers and Sisters

Question

My brother is a kung-fu freak. He is always chopping me on the neck and kicking me in the stomach. I can't hit him back because he is stronger. What should I do?

Hurting, Pittsburgh, PA

Answers

1. Kung fu is an art and not something to fool around with. Being hit in the neck with a karate or kung-fu blow can be serious. And getting kicked in the stomach is dangerous. Let your brother know this.

N.R., Seattle, WA

2. Tell your brother that experts would never chop or kick unless necessary.

L.B., Elizabeth, PA

3. I think you should take as much as you can stand. Then tell your parents. If this doesn't work, take kung-fu or karate lessons.

J.B., Rudyard, MI

4. Learn kung fu and surprise your brother. But don't hurt him.

A.D., Jeanerette, LA

5. Tell him to act his age, not his shoe size!

Sherrie, Elizabeth, PA

Question

My sister is dating a boy I really like. I can't hide my jealousy much longer. What should I do?

C.P., Columbus, OH

Answers

1. Forget about him. If he was interested in you, he'd be dating you and not your sister. Find someone else to go out with.

K.S., Van Wert, OH

2. Tell your sister how you feel about him. Then find out how he feels about you. Maybe he likes you.

A.B., Maxton, NC

3. Ask your sister to help you find your own boyfriend. If you take this boy away from your sister, you may regret it later on.

J.H., Lafayette, LA

Question

My problem is my sister. She is giving my mother lots of trouble. She's always running around. But I don't know what to tell her. Can you help me help her?

C.C., Petersburg, IL

Answers

1. Tell your sister that your mother works hard. Point out all the things that she does for both of you. The least that your sister can do is not to give her trouble. Remind your sister that your mother loves her.

C.C., Angels Camp, CA

2. I think you should tell your sister that she could end up in serious trouble. Tell her that you don't want anything bad to happen to her. Let her know that you care about her. I think that this will help a lot.

L.C.J., Davenport, FL

Question

My brother can't stand me. I've always wanted him to like me. But all he does is make fun of me and hit me. Once he threatened to stick the handle of a rake down my throat. He wasn't fooling around. He really had hate in his voice. How can I get him to be nice to me?

C.M., Aurora, IL

Answers

1. Your brother is just acting like a show-off. Ignore him for a couple of weeks. Don't do anything for him. But be quiet and polite. He'll get the hint. Then he will either ig-

nore you or be nice to you. At least he won't
hit you.

D.M., San Francisco, CA

2. Maybe your brother doesn't really hate
you. He may think that you get more attention than he gets. He's probably jealous of
you. Be nice to him and tell your parents
good things about him. Then he'll start to
show you some respect.

P.M., Kilmarnock, VA

Question

My sister is always borrowing my clothes
and asking me for favors. I usually give in.
But when I ask her to lend me something,
she always says no.

We get along well with each other most
of the time. I don't want this problem to
cause an argument. Do you know how I
could solve this?

R.T., Rio Linda, CA

Answers

1. Don't let your sister borrow any of your
clothes. If she asks you to do a favor for her,
say that you are too busy. When she realizes
that you're not her servant, she'll probably
get along better with you.

T.H., Tallmadge, OH

2. When your sister asks to borrow something, remind her that she never lends you anything. But then give her what she asks for. Show her you are not trying to be mean.

K.S., Big Lake, MN

Question

I have a brother who hides his money from me. He thinks that I will steal it. How can I convince him that I never would steal from him?

T.S., Modesto, CA

Answers

1. If you *know* that you're not going to steal his money, his attitude shouldn't upset you. Tell him to keep hiding it, and remind him to count it once in a while. This should make him see how foolish he's being.

A.M., Sycamore, IL

2. Leave your own money out to show your brother that you trust him. Offer to lend him some of your things. When he finds out that you trust him, he may start trusting you.

F.S., Cross, SC

Question

My sisters are much prettier than I am. Whenever a boy comes to see me, they flirt with him. They are attractive, and they get

all the attention. How can I make them stop?
And how can I get boys to notice me?

A.A., Pelahatchie, MS

Answers

1. Don't bring boys home when your sisters
are there. At least, not until you're really
sure that the boy likes you. Then if they flirt
with him, tell them to leave him alone.
They'll probably stop if they realize he is a
real boyfriend.

L.J.M., Fort Wayne, IN

2. Don't be jealous. Do your sisters have
boyfriends who come to the house? If so, flirt
with them. When your sisters tell you to
stop, explain the whole thing to them. If that
doesn't work, ask your mother to speak to
them. Also, let your boyfriends know that
you don't like it when *they* flirt. Let them
know there are plenty of fish in the sea.

B.M.C., Morristown, TN

Question

My brother smokes pot. I'm afraid it's
hurting his health. How can I get him to
stop?

M.C., Charlotte, NC

Answer

Tell him that it hurts you to see him hurting himself. But you can't force him to stop. He must make that decision himself. You can help by showing him that you care about him. Ask him to go places with you, and ask for his advice. This will make him feel needed and wanted. If he gets a better opinion of himself, he'll find it easier to give up pot.

L.H., Key West, FL

Question

My younger brother is pretty strong. Whenever he wants something, he hits me. Then he tells my friends that he can beat me up. I want to hit him back, but I know I'll hurt him. I can't stand his hitting much longer. What should I do?

"Big Brother"

Answers

1. Tell your parents about this. If they don't do anything, talk to your brother. If that doesn't work, hit him back. Don't hit him as hard as he hits you. Tell your friends what's going on, if they keep teasing you.

D.V., Glenolden, PA

2. If your friends are really your friends, they'll ignore him. Tell your brother that he should grow up and realize that "hitting and telling" is childish.

L.V., Monroe, VA

II

FRIENDS:

Making Friends

Question

I had a bad reputation at school last year. Now all the kids tease me so much that I can't stand it. I can't make new friends. There aren't any kids who want to risk their reputations by being friends with me. I need help badly. These kids are lying about me, because I don't act the same way any more. How can I prove that I've changed?

"Hopeless"

Answers

1. Ignore the kids who tease you. They're jealous because your reputation has changed. Show them you can take it. Prove to them

that you are living for yourself. You don't have to beg them to be your friends. Forget about them, and make friends outside of school.

B.P., Boston, GA

2. Did you think about joining some club? If you joined the school newspaper or glee club, for instance, you'd have to associate with others. Maybe then everyone would notice your new attitude toward things.

C.M., Detroit, MI

3. You can't prove to anyone that you have changed. Don't get upset when they kid you and lie about you. Just smile and keep walking. Soon they'll probably see the difference. Then they'll stop teasing you. I had the same problem. I didn't let it bother me. Now, no one teases me, and I have many new friends.

L.A.W., Grand Junction, MI

Question

I would like to know how to cure "seriousness." I love people. I would like to be jolly and make people feel comfortable. I try to make conversation, but I get turned off. I know I'm boring people. I just can't relax with others. What should I do?

Desperate, NY

Answers

1. Don't let what others think bother you. Someone will come along who shares your wants and needs. If you pretend to be someone you aren't, you may lose this person. Or worse, you may never get to know him or her. This person will be worth the lack of friends you feel now. Try to be the real you. It will help you relax.

K.J.M., Red Creek, NY

2. Calm down. Discuss different things with people. Find things you agree on. Knowing you have something in common with them should help them be friendly to you.

D.M.D., Bowie, MD

Question

I have just moved to a very nice neighborhood. Most people who live here have more money than my family has, and they do not seem friendly. I've lived here about a month, and I still don't have any friends. What can I do?

J.O., Chateaugay, Quebec

Answers

1. Forget that these people have more money than you have. Try to start a conversation with some of the kids in your class. They may want to talk with you, but they might be shy. Make the first move. Then they'll see that you are friendly.

S.S., Napa, CA

2. Join some clubs at school. Then you will get to know some people. Don't let it bother you that they have more money than you. They should like you for your personality, not for your money.

D.H., Bluffton, SC

Question

I have a problem making friends. I'm not good in gym. In fact, I can't even catch a ball. I'm 5'11" tall, and I wear a size 13 shoe. I have only one friend, and I'm very lonely. Can anyone help me?

"Troubled"

Answers

1. Everyone has some talent. You just haven't found yours yet. Try different hobbies and sports. You'll probably find something you can do well. Then people will admire you. Admiration is one way to gain friends.

"Getting There"

2. If people tease you, ignore them. Practice at some sport until you can play it well. Try not to be someone else. Be yourself.

"Thoughtful"

Question

My sisters told me about a boy in their class who has no friends. I started sending him anonymous letters because I wanted him to feel he had a friend. I'm too shy to tell him who I am. Should I keep writing to him?

"Anonymous"

Answers

1. I think it's mean to write to someone just to make him feel wanted. If he finds out the reason you're writing to him, he'll be more upset than he was before. If you really want to be friends with him, let him know who you are.

R.R.J., Roseburg, OR

2. Let him know who you are. He may think the letters are being written by someone who is kidding around. You may get tired of writing letters and stop. Then he'll think that he's done something wrong and lost his only friend. *Tell* him that you are his friend.

L.J., New York, NY

3. I'm very shy, too. I only have a few friends, and I get them by being honest. Tell this boy who you are. Otherwise he will think that the letters are a joke. I couldn't say "I love you" to my girlfriend, so I wrote her a poem. I *gave* it to her personally. Now it's easy for me to say it to her.

K.B., McMinnville, OR

Question

My best friend and I have been best friends for a long time. We do everything together. Then this other friend of mine started hanging around with us. Now he's coming between us. I wish I could tell this guy not to hang around with us. But I don't want to hurt his feelings. What should I do?

D.D., Vicksburg, MS

Answers

1. I think you should be nice to the guy. You might find out that you like him a lot. Then the three of you might have even more fun.

J.M., Port Jefferson
Station, NY

2. Your problem is not your friend. It's you! You should not have just one best friend. Don't be so dependent on one person.

S.J., Salem, IL

Question

I am very interested in space and life after death. I know a lot about these things. But I can't seem to make friends. What should I do?

Help, IN

Answers

1. Don't talk about space and life after death

all the time. Most people are more interested in things that are happening now.

R.G., Elmhurst, IL

2. You sound like a person who dreams and thinks a lot. You have to find people who also dream and think a lot. Keep looking.

K. H., Bellerville, IL

3. I share your interests. I used to think I was the only person interested in this type of stuff. But now I don't feel so alone any more. I feel that it's good to take an interest in space because we live in the space age.

Space Ager, MT

4. Get a lot of books on the topics you are interested in. Then ask some people at school if they would like to do some experiments. You could look at the stars through a telescope. Or you could hold a seance. A lot of people would like that.

G.L., Lenox Dale, MA

Whose Side Are You On?

Question

This boy broke up with my best girlfriend.

Now he wants to start dating me. How can I tell my friend that he likes me without getting her all upset? She thinks that he still likes her and that they will get back together again. I don't want to hurt her feelings. What should I do?

D.G., New Haven, CT

Answers

1. Don't go out with him, no matter how much you want to. You'll lose your friend. Boys come and go. But a relationship with a real friend is hard to find. Don't lose it.

S.R., Jennings, MO

2. I had the same problem. My best friend was very upset because I didn't tell her. I was afraid that I might hurt her feelings. Tell your friend, she might understand.

K.M., St. Louis, MO

Question

I have a friend who talks too much, and I don't know what to do. Does anyone have any advice?

B.G., Fairfax, SC

Answers

1. While you are with him, say as little as possible. When your friends see the contrast between this jabbering and your silence, he may shut up. Some musicians do this when an audience is being noisy. They stop playing or they play very softly. This makes the audience start listening.

J.O., Roundtree, NY

2. I used to talk too much. My friends told me to shut up, or just turned me off. After a while, I found myself with no friends. So I stopped talking so much. I'd tell your friend that he or she talks too much. If your friend isn't afraid to face the truth, he or she will do something about it.

L.A., Staten Island, NY

3. I would not tell her she talks too much. You might hurt her feelings. Hint around. She might get the point.

J.W., Villa Park, CA

Question

I have a lot of friends, and I have a car. This may sound good, but it causes problems. All my friends want rides all the time. But I can only take a few. When I do that, the others feel put down. I don't want to hurt anybody's feelings. Any advice for me?

J.S.L., Muncie, IN

Answers

1. I had the same problem. So now I drive

half my friends *to* school. The other half I drive home. They all understand. Good luck.

B.M., Falls, PA

2. Tell your friends they have to help pay for the gas. This should stop a few of them from wanting rides. It will also help you meet your gas bills.

M.B., Westwood, MA

Question

I'm having a real problem. Every time my friend starts to like a boy, I start to like him. Then it kills me if the boy goes out with her. She's got a great personality. She could tie any dude around her finger. What should I do about this?

Friend, Lawton, OK

Answers

1. Start looking for a guy for yourself. You'll find one.

D.W., Anaheim, CA

2. You don't like these boys as much as you think. You just don't want to feel left out. Look for another guy. Then you can all go out together.

J.P.H., Galesburg, IL

Answers

1. Ask an older girl to give your friend some advice about how she should act when boys are around. Maybe then she won't act so dumb in front of your cousin.

C.B., Cedar Mountain, NC

2. Tell her she'll impress your cousin more if she acts like herself. You might tell your cousin that she likes him. If he doesn't like her, tell her to look for someone else. She should put her hook in the ocean and pull out another one.

C.J., Philadelphia, PA

3. If she's really your friend, don't worry about hurting her feelings. Explain the way you feel, and she'll probably understand. Remind her that boys don't like girls who act immature.

M.M., Washington, D.C.

Question

Two friends of mine always seem to be stealing things from me. They don't really hate me. I guess they just do it for fun. I told my parents about their taking some money from me. My parents said, "They can't be good friends to you if they steal." But I can't believe this. I still care for both these friends very much. They are the only friends I have. What should I do?

C.E., Westfield, NJ

47

Answers

1. Tell them that you have lost some money. Say that you hope you find it soon, so you won't have to blame anyone for taking it. Then they can put the money somewhere where you can find it.

J.W., Adrian, MI

2. Tell your friends that you know they have been taking things from you. Tell them to stop it. If they don't stop, then forget all about them.

P.C., Pittsboro, NC

Question

My best friend doesn't seem to understand that I have feelings, too. When she's upset about something, I listen to her and try to help her. But when I have a problem, she says she can't help me. Should I tell her she's acting selfish?

B.G., Rio Linda, CA

Answers

1. You shouldn't tell her she's acting selfish. Maybe she doesn't trust her own judgment. She might get upset if she gives you advice and it doesn't work. Try telling your problems to a teacher or your parents.

T.W.

2. I had the same problem with my friend. One day, I told her she *had* to listen to me. That made her realize what she had been doing to me. Now we talk about my problems, as well as hers. Don't tell your friend she is selfish. Maybe she doesn't realize how she's acting.

S.K., LaPlata, MD

Question

I have a friend who always talks about people behind their backs. She seems to enjoy "cutting up" others. How can I stop her from doing this without hurting her feelings?

L.N., Mississauga, Ontario

Answers

1. Tell your friend, as kindly as you can, to stop this. Otherwise you'll stop being her friend. If this doesn't work, find another friend.

S.S., Norwalk, CT

2. Ask your friend how she would feel if someone talked about *her* behind *her* back. You may hurt her feelings. But this may help her realize how unfair she is being.

"A Friend," Greenbush, MN

Question

My friend's boyfriend gets very angry

when they argue. He calls her names and tells her to give him back his ring. But as soon as she starts crying he says, "I'm only kidding." Do you think she should keep dating him?

"A Friend," Wilkes Barre, PA

Answers

1. Your friend should break up with this boy. It sounds as if he just wants to make her unhappy. Maybe he wants her to prove that she really cares for him. But he could have a real problem. Some people can only be happy when they make someone else unhappy.

Tell your girlfriend to talk to him. If he can't give her a good reason for his actions, she should drop him.

B.Y., Tappahannock, VA

2. You shouldn't get involved in your friend's love life. Maybe you like this boy yourself. Is that why you're so interested in how he gets along with your friend? Maybe you want them to break up.

D.D., Bellerose, NY

Question

I belong to this club. Some of the members have been putting me down lately. I didn't know why at first. But one of my friends told me later. He said that everybody in the club wanted to beat up the white students in school. Should I stick with the club or quit?

S.R.

Answers

1. I suggest that you drop out of the club. But stay friendly with everyone, no matter what color they are. If you think your friends are getting too serious about the fighting, talk to your counselor. Or talk to the principal.

D.M.S., Lake Charles, LA

2. If you don't want to get into trouble, try to persuade the club not to fight the white students. If that doesn't work, then quit.

D.N., Tolano, IL

3. I feel that you should stay in the club. If you leave, they might think you are for the white students. Then they might beat you up. As a black student, I would stay in the club. But it's your life. Good luck.

R.H., Poughkeepsie, NY

Question

I have two friends who don't like each other, but they both want to be friends with me. I want to spend time with each of them. What should I do?

D.B., Rio Linda, CA

Answers

1. Here is how I worked out the same problem. I told both friends I liked them equally, and I would see each one every other day. You might try this.

D.O., Metamora, IL

2. Have your friends visit you together. Try to find out why they don't like each other. After a talk, it may turn out that all three of you can be friends.

R.N., Midwest City, OK

Question

My friend takes drugs. She doesn't know I know this. Some people say that I should report her. Other people say I shouldn't. What should I do?

"Curious," Montreal, Quebec

Answers

1. Don't report your friend. Talk to her and tell her taking drugs is not a good idea.

C.B., Victoria, B.C., Canada

2. Don't report her. If you do, your other friends won't trust you. Just spend less time with her. And make sure you don't get hooked.

"A Friend," Hatfield, PA

3. If you were really her friend, you would report her. The people you report her to will help her. There are many services that can help your friend with a drug problem.

A.Y., Van Wert, OH

4. Don't report her. Try to get her to go to a drug rehabilitation center. She might tell the people there why she takes drugs. They will be able to help her. And she'll still trust you as her friend. She'll know you care.

C.C., Troupsburg, NY

Losing Friends

Question

I have a friend who used to be my best friend. Now she is turning against me. She is telling other people all about me. I don't know what to do about it. Every time I try to talk to her, she just frowns. What should I do?

E.S., Cupertino, CA

Answers

1. I had this problem, and I think I have an answer. Ignore the bad things she's done to you. Try being nice to her. Give her a present on her birthday, but don't expect one back. Don't try to make her your best friend again. Maybe she thinks you've changed, too.

P.A.M., Lowell, MA

2. Tell this girl it's okay if she doesn't want to be your friend any more. But tell her she should stop talking about you. Don't make a big thing out of it. Make new friends, and forget her. She's probably doing this just to bother you.

C.F., Pasadena, CA

Question

My friends think I'm dumb and a goody-goody. This is just because I don't cuss. And I don't do things that hurt other people. I've tried to make other friends, but I like the friends I now have — except for what I wrote about. What should I do?

S.V., CA

Answers

1. If they are real friends, they're just teasing. After a while, they'll get tired and stop. Stay the way you are. Don't be a coward.

K.K., Santa Fe, NM

2. It sounds as if you *are* a bit of a goody-goody. If you don't want to swear, that's your business. But why make a big thing out of what your friends do? Are you sure you haven't been hard on them?

J.W., Chapel Hill, NC

Question

I have a friend who thinks he is funny. He tells all these stupid jokes. They are not funny. Should I tell him? I don't want to hurt his feelings. But he's losing all his friends.

L.S., Northglen, CO

Answers

1. You should tell him, because the joke is on him. He will lose all his friends. Someday, someone will really hurt his feelings. They'll tell him the truth in a mean way. You could do it in a nice way.

R.R., Phoenix, AZ

2. I don't think you can tell him without hurting his feelings. At first, try dropping a few hints. If he's smart, he'll take the hints. If not, you'll have to talk to him. He may not like it at first. But, in the end, he'll be glad.

V.W., Brandon, MS

3. When he tells his jokes, don't laugh. That should tell him something. He's probably just trying to get attention. Talk to him. Make him feel important. Then he won't have to act like a clown all the time.

E.J., Pelahatchie, MS

Question

All the kids at school seem to dislike me. They have given me a mean nickname, and they say I'm crazy. I can't help it. I have a habit of talking to myself. The kids say I drive them crazy. Please help me.

Nicknamed, Boston, MA

Answers

1. If I were you, I'd tell those kids to mind their own business. At the same time, try to break the habit of talking to yourself.

"Solver," Kansas City, KS

2. Instead of talking to yourself, talk to someone else. I'm sure everyone doesn't hate you. Sometimes kids give people nicknames for attention. Aren't they noticing you?

N.S., Gainesville, FL

Question

I'm a guy who is having trouble with two other guys. They were both my friends, and I introduced them to each other. Now they don't want to be friends with me. What should I do?

J.S., Fort Wayne, IN

Answer

I had the same problem. At first, I was

really upset. Then I realized that they were not my true friends. If they were, they wouldn't ignore me. I decided to forget about them. But I still said hello to them, so they wouldn't know I was upset. If I were you, I'd find different friends.

T.R., Stormville, NY

Question

I don't smoke except when I'm around people who do smoke. Then it's hard not to. I know smoking is bad for you. But how do you say "no" when everyone else is smoking?

M.K.B., Decatur, IL

Answers

1. Just tell your friends you have to quit. If they put you down for it, you have the wrong kind of friends.

J.R., Warren, NJ

2. Why let people tell you what to do? You have to make up your mind that you want to quit. Then do it!

G.T., Kansas City, KS

Question

A boy in one of my classes is really a pest. He's always trying to sell things to people.

His voice is so loud that it's hard to ignore him. I don't like going to this class any more.

My friends agree with me, but we don't know what to do. How can we keep this boy quiet?

F.D., Jamaica, NY

Answers

1. Since this boy is always trying to sell you things, buy something from him. But tell him that if he keeps being noisy, you'll never buy anything from him again. Then he might stop bothering you.

D.A., Anderson, IN

2. Ignore this boy. Don't buy anything he is selling. Tell him that if he wants to have friends, he should lower his voice. Ask him to sell things after school. Then he won't upset the whole class. You may think this is cruel. But think of how many friends he'll lose if he keeps annoying people.

D.S., Dunnsville, VA

Question

I have very nice friends, but they are boring. All they want to do is sit and talk. I'd rather be active. Ice skating is very cheap. And there are so many other things to do. I do them alone, but that isn't much fun. What should I do?

Help, Buffalo, NY

Answers

1. Maybe you just haven't found something that your friends like to do. If you drive, there are lots of places to go and things to do. If you don't have a car, you can ride a bike. Keep suggesting things to them.

K.R., Galesburg, IL

2. If your friends are too lazy to have fun, forget them. Join a club or a school team. Then you will meet people who are interested in the same things you are.

T.V., Eaton Rapids, MI

III

DATING:

Getting Together

Question

My boyfriend is crazy about me, but when I see him, I play hard to get. I tell him I'm dating other guys, even though I'm not. I really like my boyfriend, and I want to spend more time with him. How can I stop acting this way and be myself?

P.F., Charlotte, NC

Answers

1. If you keep acting this way, he'll probably drop you. Spend more time with him, and just be yourself.

C.O., Crown Point, IN

2. I don't think you like your boyfriend as much as you say you do. When you play hard to get, you're hurting his feelings. Think about this, and you may start acting differently.

"Someone Who Knows"

Question

I am very jealous of my boyfriend. He acts the same way about me. We know we shouldn't feel this way, but what should we do?

C.A., Reading, PA

Answer

Try to understand that when he talks to another girl, he's just having a conversation. He should try to understand the same about you. If you love each other, then you should trust each other.

P.T., Hundred, WV

Question

I am going out with a boy who doesn't like Spanish or black people. A year ago, I was going with a Spanish guy. I liked him a lot. How can I make my boyfriend see that he shouldn't feel this way?

M.B., MA

Answers

1. Ask your boyfriend how he would feel if he were rejected just because of his race or group. Tell him that some day he might need a good friend. And that friend might be black or Spanish.

D.M., Winston-Salem, NC

2. If you really like him, you should like him for better or for worse. Maybe he and your old boyfriend could get together.

Dot, Detroit, MI

3. Quit him. The longer you stay with him, the more he will embarrass and hurt you.

W.K., Sharpsburg, MD

Question

My boyfriend hardly ever talks to me, except over the phone. I feel weird when I talk to him by phone because *I* call *him*. He seems to like it when I call him, though. Should a girl call a guy?

P.T., Ballico, CA

Answers

1. This guy sounds as if he isn't really interested in you. How could he be your boyfriend if he hardly talks to you? I think you should break up with him. I know guys who act the

way he does. All they do is make people unhappy.

D.P., Greensboro, NC

2. Stop calling him for a while. Then he may start to call you. I tried this with my boyfriend, and it worked.

P.L.C., Jacksonville, NC

Question

I have a girlfriend, and I really like her. But she gets angry when other girls talk to me. I can't help it if they like me. And I'm not the kind of guy who would be rude to girls. But now, even my friends who are boys seem to think this is wrong. I asked one guy to share his locker with me. He said, "Share it with a girl." What should I do?

Popular, Albany, NY

Answers

1. I am a girl, and I know how your girlfriend feels. But you two must be honest. Tell her it's only human nature for a guy to be *friendly* with girls. And make sure you don't mind her being friendly with other guys.

S.A., Murfreesboro, TN

2. Your girlfriend would feel better if you gave her more attention. Make her realize how much you like her.

"Experienced," Ray, ND

Question

Whenever I take my girlfriend out, her brother comes along. Her mother makes him. I don't mind the brother. But I'd like to be alone with my girlfriend some of the time. What should I do about this?

S.G., Pelahatchie, MS

Answers

1. Get a girl for her brother. If the brother likes a girl, he won't have time to tag along with you.

A friend, Grand Rapids, MI

2. Maybe your girlfriend's mother doesn't trust you. Have a short talk with her. Tell her you'd like to be alone with her daughter some of the time. Always act polite. Don't stay out too late. She may begin to trust you. Then she will leave you alone.

L.P., Troy, NY

Question

How can I get my girlfriend to understand that I love her? I'm always nice to her, and I try to do things for her. But she never tells me she cares for me. She goes out with me a lot, so she must like me.

R.T., Alligator, MS

Answers

1. Tell her that you love her. Being nice to her won't let her know how deeply you really feel. Talk it over with her. You may find out that you both feel the same way.

P.A.L., Garden City, LA

2. Don't be afraid to ask her if she loves you. She might say yes. If she doesn't, at least you know where you stand.

"A Friend"

Question

I told this boy that I like him. Now he completely ignores me. I want him to understand that he doesn't have to go out with me. But I would still like to talk to him and be his friend. How can I straighten this out?

P.M.G., Los Angeles, CA

Answers

1. Guys usually get turned off when girls take the first step. Talk to him again. Let him know that you just want to be his friend. You're not asking him to go steady.

A.O., Miami, FL

2. I'm a guy who thinks you should ignore *him* for a while. Then he'll probably start paying attention to you.

J.H., Bluffton, OH

3. Find out why he's ignoring you. Either he doesn't like you, or he's teasing you. You might ask one of his friends to find out why he's acting this way. Give it a little time, and you may find the answer.

M.M., New York, NY

Question

My boyfriend rides motorcycles. I'm afraid he is going to be badly hurt. I tried to talk to him about this. But all he says is, "Don't worry, I'll be okay." What should I do?

C.C., Aliquippa, PA

Answers

1. If your boyfriend is a sensible person, he will be all right. He shouldn't try fancy tricks on his bike. He shouldn't race, either. I broke my leg when I was in a race. Tell your boyfriend to wear riding boots, as well as a helmet.

G.J., Nashville, TN

2. Go to a traffic court and ask for some pictures of people who have been in motorcycle accidents. After your boyfriend sees these pictures, he may not want to ride his bike anymore. Or, if he still wants to ride his bike, he'll probably be very careful in the future.

M.B., Miami, FL

3. My boyfriend is a careful rider, but he still has accidents. When he gets hurt, I feel the way you do. But he enjoys the sport, so I won't ask him to give it up.

I used to be jealous of the time he spent on his bike. Now he's teaching me to ride, and I'm enjoying it.

D.S., East Moline, IL

4. Two years ago, my boyfriend bought a motorcycle. One week later, he was killed when he crashed into a car. The driver of the car was killed, too.

I begged my boyfriend not to buy that motorcycle. He didn't listen. Please talk to your boyfriend again. Tell him what happened to my boyfriend. Maybe he'll listen to you.

"Anonymous"

Question

My girlfriend wanted to go steady, and I didn't. I felt we should date other people, too. Now she has given me up completely. How can I get her to date me again — without going steady?

M.Z.M., Orange, NJ

Answers

1. Go out with other girls for a while. Then ask her out again. Maybe she'll go out with you when she sees that she's not the only girl you can date.

2. Ask her why she won't go out with you now, if she wanted to go steady with you a short time ago. Tell her you care for her, but you're just not ready to go steady. Maybe she'll start dating you again.

B.B., Williamsburg, VA

Question

I really like this guy. He's dated me a few times. How can I get him to ask me to go steady?

T.H., Apple Valley, MN

Answers

1. You can't "get" him to ask you to go steady. He has to make that decision himself. Pressuring him will only make things worse. Play it cool, and don't act as though you're going after him. Just be his friend. Maybe something good will come out of your friendship.

A.F., Seattle, WA

2. There are two qualities that I look for in the girls I date. These are neatness and intelligence. When this guy takes you out again, make sure that you look cool and act cool.

Then there's a chance that he'll ask you to
go steady.

M.W., Dayton, OH

3. All you can do is wait for him to ask you.
In the meantime, go out with other guys.

"Friends," Newport, OR

Question

My girlfriend wants me to join the track
team at school. The coach wants me to join
the baseball team, which I'd like to do. But
I don't want to lose my girlfriend. Any suggestions?

E.D., Camden, SC

Answers

1. Join the team *you* want to join. If your
girlfriend breaks off with you, she probably
didn't care very much for you in the first
place.

L.S., Akron, OH

2. Pick the sport you like best. When you
enjoy something, you usually do it well. Explain this to your girlfriend. If she really
cares about you, she'll understand.

W.W., Maxton, NC

Question

I met a guy this summer, and I like him a

lot. But he lives about 400 miles away from here. It's hard to believe that he isn't dating other girls. I don't go out with other guys because he writes me and says he still likes me. But what should I do until I see him again?

T.S., Kalamazoo, MI

Answers

1. Don't go steady with a guy who lives that far away. He's probably dating other girls. When you see him again, go out with him. Meanwhile, date people who go to school with you.

J.T., Indian Hill, OH

2. Write to him, and tell him that you like him. But remind him that you're too young to just sit home. Tell him that you want to go out and have fun. You'll both probably change a lot between now and the next time you see each other. By that time, you may not have anything in common. So don't tie yourself down waiting for him. Date other people.

T.T., Imperial, TX

3. If you like him a lot, you should be able to trust him. I think you should wait for him.

D.L., Burlington, KS

Question

I have asked a few girls out, but they always say no. I don't understand why. Now I met a girl I really like. She said she couldn't go out with me because she had another date. I think she was telling the truth. I don't want to ruin this because she may like me, too. How can I get her to go out with me and tell her about my feelings?

M.M., Ponder, TX

Answers

1. Start a conversation with her. Then ask her for a date. Don't try to impress her. Just be yourself.

D.H., Hundred, WV

2. Don't rush her. Most girls like to date more than one boy. If she goes out with you, don't tell her how you feel about her right away. After a while, she'll know.

T.C., Muncie, IN

Question

I just broke off with my boyfriend, but he won't leave me alone. Wherever I go, he goes. If I'm with a boy I like, he finds an excuse for seeing me.

I think he wants me to go out with him

again. But I know that wouldn't work. How can I get rid of him?

"Bothered," Montreal, Quebec

Answers

1. Tell him to stop following you around. Say that you will be his friend; but he must give you time to be alone with other people.

M.M., Lincoln Park, MI

2. You should be flattered he thinks so much of you. Go out with him again. Maybe he's changed.

J.K., Metamora, IL

Question

I have a problem with my boyfriend. He hardly ever calls me. When he does, he hardly talks to me. Most of the time, he wants to talk to my cousin. All they talk about is cars, cars, cars! I feel that he wants to call it quits, but doesn't know how to put it. What should I do?

S.W., Oakland, CA

Answers

1. I think you should learn about cars. If that does not help, tell him what's on your mind. If he does not change, let your cousin have him.

B.C., Pasadena, CA

2. It seems to me that you and your boyfriend don't have enough in common. Get interested in what he's interested in. See how much longer you can talk about something you both like.

C.A., Indianapolis, IN

3. I think you should talk to him. Ask him if he wants to break up. Maybe you should suggest breaking up. Just be friends for a while. Maybe he'll change his way of acting. Or maybe you'll find someone you like better.

L.V., Miami, FL

Question

I've gone with this girl several times. Each time, she has broken up with me. I was angry the last time when she wanted to go back with me. But I went back anyway. Now I'm angry again. But I still want to go with her. One reason we break up so much is that we have small problems. Instead of talking about them, she breaks up. What can we *both* do about *our* problems?

Very Much in Love, OH

Answers

1. I had the same problem. Talk to your girlfriend. Decide on a solution. Do this when she isn't angry.

L.N., Edmonton, Alberta

2. Maybe she thinks you're not someone she can tell her troubles to. Make her feel she can trust you. Then she may talk about her problems.

J.B., Kenbridge, VA

3. I bet you're doing more tolerating than loving. This girl has you under her thumb. But since you want to stay with her, I have two suggestions. First, write letters to each other listing your likes and dislikes. Second, take a vacation from each other. Then maybe she will value you more. If not, she isn't worth it.

K.M., Rochester, NY

Question

I like this guy a lot. And he likes me. He told his friend that he likes me. He asks me out, and we have a good time. But in school or when we are not on a date, it's different. He acts as if he doesn't know me. How can I get him to talk to me?

J.M.W.

Answers

1. I have had the same problem. I was going with a guy. When we were on a date, he was fine. But as soon as he was with a bunch of guys, I just didn't exist to him. So I decided to do the same thing. We went on like that for a while, and we both hated it. Now we stop and talk, no matter how many people are around.

J.W., London Falls, IL

2. Maybe he doesn't talk to you because he's afraid of people watching. He's afraid that they will tease him. When you want to talk to him, tap him on the shoulder. Then go some place where no one is watching. Or tell him you want to talk to him later. And tell him where you will be. Pretty soon, he should come out of his shell.

K.F.H., St. Paul, MN

3. Cool off, friend. Most guys don't like to be around girls at school. Some guys are embarrassed, especially around their friends. Don't feel bad.

L.G., Bethany, OK

Question

I have a problem about my boyfriend. I want to break up with him, but I don't know how. I am shy and afraid.

R.R., Westfield, NJ

Answers

1. I had the same problem. My advice is to quit him. The longer you stay with him, the more it will hurt him when you do break up.

Also, if you break up with him, you might then think you still like him. But don't be upset. It's just that you'll be jealous if you see him with another girl. But you'll get over it. I did.

K.M., Chicago, IL

2. Tell him your reasons for wanting to break up. It usually isn't one-sided. Afterwards, try to stay friends.

L.B., San Francisco, CA

Question

The girl I go out with lies all the time. She can't tell the truth about anything. This can be a real problem. What should I do?

B.K., Bowie, MD

Answers

1. The girl doesn't seem like the right kind of girl for you. If she really cared for you, she wouldn't keep telling you lies. If you stay with her, you are just asking for trouble. Someone who lies all the time isn't very trustworthy.

C.Q., Forestville, MD

2. Be honest with her. Tell her you won't go out with her any more if she keeps telling lies. If she gets mad, she doesn't really care that much for you.

P.D., Duncan, SC

Question

The boy I go out with is very cute. He's a real girl-getter. But that's not the problem. I'm not jealous about him. He's the jealous one. If a boy even looks as if he might look at me, he gets mad. What should I do?

S.L., Hackensack, NJ

Answers

1. Are you going steady with him? If you aren't, he doesn't have the right to get jealous. If you are, maybe you shouldn't go steady. Maybe it's too much for him.

D.B., Campbell, CA

2. You should tell him that you like him a lot. Tell him he doesn't have to worry about anyone else. Show him that you mean it. And never hide anything from him.

K.R., Galesburg, IL

3. Have you tried talking to the boy? It might help you both to trust each other more.

J.G., Duncanville, TX

Question

I am going with two girls. They both live out of town. I love them both, but I have to drop one of them. The bus fare has gone up.

I can't afford it. But I don't know which one
to drop. How should I decide?

R.L., Morristown, TN

Answers

1. My advice is to call or write to both of
them. Explain the whole situation. The one
who understands is the one you should keep.
But you know how girls are. One of them is
bound to quit you.

V.W., Shreveport, WA

2. You should pick the one who lives closer.
Then it won't cost so much.

S.R.N., Galesburg, IL

3. Drop both girls. You're crazy to spend all
your time and money on buses. Find a girl in
your own town.

E.M., Tampa, FL

4. I think you should take a good look at
yourself. You may be too immature to be
going out with girls. You should be worried
about the girls' feelings, not bus fares. You
probably don't like the idea of being tied
down. Maybe that's why you are going with
two girls at one time.

A.D., Clinton, CT

Question

I'm 13, and my boyfriend is 16. Whenever
we go out, I have to pay my own way. What

do other people think of this? Should boys pay for their dates, or not?

N.M., White Plains, NY

Answers

1. If he really likes you, I think he would pay your way. He's just using you. Maybe you've done something to make him mad. Try talking it over with him.

Y.S., Bronx, NY

2. Yes, boys should pay for their dates. People will think you are a fool if you pay your own way.

D.N., Columbia, SC

3. If he really wants to take you out, he should enjoy spending the money.

S.G., Columbia, SC

4. I think boys should pay. But maybe your boyfriend doesn't have enough money. If that's true, try going on dates that don't cost much. Or else stay home until he can save up enough money.

P.M., Bronx, NY

5. If your boyfriend doesn't have a job, you should pay, too. Talk to him. Find out if he really doesn't have the money.

C.A.P.

6. I know of many girls who pay their own way. One reason is that boys have a hard time finding jobs. Is it more important that he pay for you, or that he loves you? If you really care about him, you would be willing to pay *his* way, too.

K.J.M., Red Creek, NY

Question

I am 16, and my boyfriend is 20. We want to get married now, but my parents say no. They want me to finish school first. I think they are old fashioned. We have talked to them, but they still say no. What can we do?

Help!, Los Angeles, CA

Answers

1. In my opinion, marriage at your age won't work. I've known three couples who got married when they were very young. All three have split up. They just weren't mature enough. Many young marriages fail because of this. Good luck.

H.K., Norristown, PA

2. Your parents are right. It's hard trying to finish school later. It's also expensive. And you need to finish school if you want to get a good job.

R.K., DeSoto, TX

3. If you both love each other, you should elope. Maybe you could get married and keep

it secret for a while. Your parents will probably approve once you are actually married.

D.K., Boise, ID

4. Whatever you do, don't quit school. I know what I'm talking about. My mother is 39, and she is just finishing school. It is really rough on her. Even if your husband has a good job now, things might be different in 10 years. What if he died and left you with children? This is what my mother had to face.

A Good Friend

5. If this guy really loves you, he'll wait for you. So finish school before you get married.

Dugi, Conshohocken, PA

6. The best thing to do is to finish school. But if you can't, then get married anyway. Tell your parents that it's your life, not theirs. If you get married now, maybe you could go to night school.

L.C., Los Angeles, CA

Question

I am 17, and I have been going with a guy who is 15. My parents say I'm too old for him. Do you agree? He's really the only thing that matters to me. I don't think age matters. But how can I convince my parents?

N.J.R., Winsted, CT

Answers

1. Tell your parents that our generation is different from theirs. Age isn't important to us. If you really like this boy, that's all that matters.

M.W., Ann Arbor, MI

2. It all depends on this guy. Does he act like a little kid? Or does he act like someone your age? If he isn't mature, then your parents are right.

M.E.T., Bloomington, TN

3. I agree with your parents. You *are* too old to be going with a 15-year-old. Go to some dances, and try to find an older guy. Someone older will mean much more to you than this 15-year-old.

P.H., Troupsburg, NY

Question

A girl I like very much is going with another guy. She always talks to me. Should I ask her if she likes me — or forget about her?

"Deeply in Love"

Answers

1. If she talks to you, she must like you as a friend. Keep talking to her and being nice to

her. Be yourself. Maybe after a while, she'll
realize how you feel about her.

C.W., Holyoke, MA

2. Forget about her. There are other fish in
the sea.

J.R., Crown Point, IN

3. Tell her how you feel. Then she might
start going out with you as a girlfriend.
Good luck.

"Advice"

Question

I am 16 years old, and my boyfriend is 21.
We love each other very much. My mother
wants me to break up with him because he is
black and I'm not. Should I keep on seeing
him? Or should I listen to my mother? I need
some help.

"Confused"

Answers

1. I'm black and my mother has told me that
she will not be pleased with me if I date
white guys. It sounds to me that your mother
told you some time ago she didn't want you
to date black guys. You may be going out
with him because you love him. But you
might also be trying to defy your mother.
Has your mother met him? Does she know

what kind of a person he really is? If not, maybe you should bring him home. If that doesn't work, you should probably stop seeing him for a while. If it's really love, it will last until the trouble ends.

P.A.A., Summit, NJ

2. Decide for yourself. If you love him, that's all that matters. It's your life, not your mother's. Color doesn't make any difference. If you love someone and care for him, that's what counts.

K.M., St. Louis, MO

3. I come from an interracial family, so I am both black and white. I'm going out with a white guy and my skin color is brown. If you really love him, keep going out with him. Try talking it over with your mother, maybe she'll understand.

D.M., Boston, MA

4. Your mother probably has her reasons for feeling this way. Take her advice. At 16 you probably don't really know what you want.

M.L., Brevard, NC

5. My parents are both of different races, and I love them both. Keep seeing him. You won't regret it. My parents are very happy with each other. When they got married in the 50's, many people thought they were

crazy. But now people don't feel this way any more.

"Understands"

6. You should keep seeing him if you care about him. Sometimes, parents are over-protective. Have a mother-daughter talk with your mother. Tell her how you feel about him. Tell her that color doesn't mean anything to you. Make sure you talk to her in a responsible and respectful voice.

A.D.W., Charleston, SC

7. My cousin married a black guy. They are really happy. You should be able to go out with this guy if you want to. But talk to your mother. Try to see her reasons for the way she feels. If you ever marry this guy you must realize that your children won't belong to either race. They may get hassled about this and not have any friends.

"Helpful"

Question

I like a girl in my class a lot. But I'm too shy to talk to her. Every time she talks to me, I start to blush. What should I do to get to know her better?

C.M., Beaver Falls, PA

Answers

1. Why don't you call her on the phone?

Then if you blush she won't know about it.
When you call her, tell her how you feel.
Tell her that you're shy. If this doesn't work,
you could write her a note.

G.V., Lincoln Park, MI

2. Half your problem is solved because *she*
talks to *you*. Now try not to be self-conscious, and have a little more confidence in
yourself. Don't worry about blushing. Once
you start talking to her, you'll probably forget all about it.

K.L., Torrance, CA

Question

My boyfriend spends too much time with
his car. He washes it, waxes it, and takes
pictures of it. I'm starting to think he likes
his car more than he likes me. When I tell
him this, he says I'm being silly. How can I
get him to pay more attention to me?

K.J.R., Galax, VA

Answer

My boyfriend used to act the same way
toward his car. I finally started asking him
questions about the car. I would even help
him clean it. Soon he started talking to me
about many other subjects — things we had
never talked about before. I was no longer

just his girlfriend. I had become his friend, as well.

R.S., Crete, IL

Question

My boyfriend has a 16-year-old sister. Whenever he has an argument with her, he has a fight with me. I know that she upsets him. But I don't think he should take it out on me. How can I help to control his anger?

J.R.W., San Diego, CA

Answers

1. Tell him you want to be a friend, not a doormat. Tell him to *talk* to you, not *yell* at you, when he is angry with his sister.

N.A.N., Glenn Dale, MD

2. Tell him to walk away from his sister when she starts arguing with him. Explain to his sister about the way he acts after they have an argument. She will probably understand and stop fighting with him.

S.Y.J., Clearwater, FL

Question

My best girlfriend took my boyfriend away from me. What can I do about it?

K.H., Randolph, NY

Answers

1. If a boy doesn't want to be taken away, he won't go. Your boyfriend probably likes your girlfriend more than he likes you. There isn't much you can do about it. Just pretend it doesn't bother you, and be nice to him. Maybe he'll feel foolish for what he's done.

S.O., Tulsa, OK

2. Maybe he didn't like you that much in the first place. Then again, he might come back to you when he finds out what this girl is like. Meanwhile, try to forget about him and keep busy.

C.H., Breckenridge, MI

Question

My boyfriend and I are going together for the third time. We broke up twice because he lied to me. Each time, he told me he had stopped using drugs. Later, I found out he was still using them. Now he tells me he's off drugs again. We haven't seen each other for a month. I love him and I want to marry him. But I want to trust him. How can I be sure he's telling me the truth now?

D.K.B., Savannah, GA

Answers

1. Don't see this boy again until he straight-

ens out his life. Ask him to go to a drug rehabilitation center. When you are sure that he has given up drugs completely, go out with him again.

S.W., Baltimore, MD

2. Ask your boyfriend why he lies to you. Then try to help him stop using drugs. Don't keep breaking up with him, because this could make him feel tense. He might get so depressed, he'll start using drugs again.

T.L.B., Carmichaels, PA

3. Maybe your boyfriend has told you the truth about his drug problem. He may be trying to quit, but he may need help. Tell him you really love him and you want to help him. If he doesn't accept your help, forget about him.

J.E., Bar Harbor, ME

Question

I've been going out with a boy for six months. I like him very much. But now I think he's tired of me. When I ask him if we should break up, he tells me I'm acting silly. But he isn't acting the way he used to. How can I keep him interested in me?

T.J., Fairborn, OH

Answers

1. Stop seeing him for a few days. This

should make him notice you again. If this doesn't work, find a new boyfriend.

B.R., Holly Hill, SC

2. *Stop* asking him if he wants to break up with you. You're only boring him by asking him this all the time. If he wants to drop you, he will. There isn't anything you can do to change his mind.

B.F., Baltimore, MD

Question

My problem is that this boy in my class likes me. But I don't like him. He has been writing me notes that say, "I love you." What can I tell him without hurting his feelings?

C.M.

Answers

1. I would politely ask him not to write any more notes. If he doesn't stop, throw the notes away without reading them.

B.M., Fork Union, VA

2. Tell him you already have a boyfriend. But tell him in a nice way. If you hurt his feelings, tell him you're sorry. If that doesn't work, ignore him.

A.T., Costa Mesa, CA

3. When he sends you notes, rip them up before you read them. Or, why don't you send

him notes? This might scare him off. Anyway, why don't you like him? Think about it. You might find out that you really *do* like him.

M.S., Jennings, MO

Question

I'm going with a guy who is in the Army. He been in for about six months. I still care for him, but I am meeting other guys. Should I go out with them? My mother says it would be wrong.

D.L.M., Delaware, OH

Answers

1. I have the same problem. My boyfriend is in the Marines. I promised to wait for him. But I met other guys. My mother, like your mother, said it would be wrong to date others. So I wrote to my boyfriend about the problem. He wrote back and said he was very hurt. I love him a lot, so I stopped dating others. I think you should do the same.

D.S., Clarksburg, WV

2. You should go out with other guys, but don't get serious. This way, you won't hurt the guy in the Army. And you won't hurt any guys here. You have to be honest. Then you'll have fun, and you won't feel guilty. And you'll probably find out that you still care for him the most.

S.N., Cincinnati, OH

Question

My girlfriend just broke off with me. She wanted to go out all the time, and I didn't have enough time for that. When we did go out, all our friends would come with us. Neither of us liked that. She also said she was dating other people while she was going with me. She thinks this shouldn't change my feelings for her. But I am very depressed. Should I forget about her?

F.O.S., Lancaster, CA

Answers

1. I think you should forget about her. She should not have dated other people while going with you. Also, she should not expect you to spend all your time with her.

D.F., West Jefferson, OH

2. I don't think it was right for her to date other guys. But she seems to want to go out more often than you. Maybe the two of you could still date each other and other people, too. This way, she could date as much as she wanted — without lying to you. At the same time, you wouldn't feel forced to take her out all the time.

K.W., Andrews, TX

Question

I have *two* girlfriends. Even though one

of them is dating another guy, I don't want to drop her. The other girl is just dating me, and I like her a lot. Should I keep seeing them both — or drop one?

A.L., Coraopolis, PA

Answers

1. You are being unfair to both girls. Make up your mind before one of them gets hurt. Maybe you should drop both of them and find another girlfriend.

B.J., Lansdale, PA

2. If you're doing fine with both, why stop? But you do have a choice. How about picking the girl you enjoy being with more?

R.G., Jennings, MO

3. Just be friends with the girl who has another boyfriend. Keep seeing the girl who doesn't have a boyfriend. You could get to know the guy the other girl is dating. Maybe you could be friends with him, too.

M.O., Rochester, NY

Question

I like this guy, but I don't know if he likes me. Whenever he's around, I'm afraid I'll say the wrong thing. How can I let him know I like him?

"Afraid"

Answer

Try talking to him. Don't be afraid that you'll say the wrong thing. Remember, he's not perfect, either. But be careful not to hurt his feelings. Be yourself. Here are some fun things to do to catch his attention:

Write a message with a felt-tipped pen on a piece of cardboard. Cut it into a jigsaw puzzle and mail it to him.

Leave a heart-shaped cookie on his doorstep.

Remove the fortune from a fortune cookie. Replace the message with one of your own.

Take a picture of something he likes. Have the picture blown up to poster size.

Nominate him for school office, and offer to be his campaign manager.

Ask him to teach you how to draw, ride a skateboard, or whatever he does best.

Good luck.

"Helpful Hints"

IV

MISCELLANEOUS:

School

Question

Our teacher tries to act like Fonzie on TV's *Happy Days*. This embarrasses us. How should we react to his behavior?

"Upset Class"

Answers

1. If your teacher cracks a joke, don't laugh. If he says, "Haaay," keep on doing your work. After a while, he may realize that he's being foolish.

M.L., New Berlin, WI

2. You might speak to the teacher or leave him a note. The message could be: "We come

to school to learn, not to watch the Fonz. Please change this habit, and we will change our attitudes for the better."

M.E.B., Seattle, WA

Question

I don't know if I should stay in school or quit. I had planned to get married and go overseas with my husband. But if I do, I won't be able to finish school. What should I do?

S.B., Duncanville, TX

Answers

1. I think I would go with my husband. That's where a wife belongs, not thousands of miles away from him. Today there are schools you can go to at any age. You could go back to school whenever you came back to this country.

D.S., Kaplan, LA

2. I think I'd stay in school. If you are worried about your education, talk to your boyfriend. Ask him to wait for you to finish. If he doesn't want to wait, drop him. Find another boyfriend. There are always more guys.

T.S., Sault Ste. Marie, MI

3. Talk with your school counselor. See if you can get extra credit to finish high school before the rest of your class. If that's not possible, I wouldn't let school get ahead of my personal life.

R.L., Pelahatchie, MI

4. Don't be a dummy the way I was. Finish school. Then get married. You'll find out in the future that it will pay off. Good luck.

A.P., Lincolndale, NY

Question

Some guy at school keeps taking my money. How can I get him to stop stealing from me?

S.D., Albany, NY

Answers

1. Keep your money with you all the time. Put a *good* lock on your locker, and leave your money there when you play sports. If you don't have a locker, ask the gym teacher to hold the money for you. When this guy sees that he can't get anything from you, he'll look for another victim. If none of this works, tell a teacher about his problem.

N.N., Imperial, TX

2. Ask a close friend to hold your money for you until this guy stops bothering you.

B.T., Maxton, NC

Question

I have a problem with my schoolmates.

They think I take drugs, and I don't! It all started when we moved to this little town. My dad is a dentist. He has a beard and long hair. The little old ladies here started to gossip. They said he is a hippie. They said he is pushing drugs. When I was absent from school, a rumor started that I take drugs. I keep getting teased, and I can't stand it any more. Please help.

Confused, WI

Answers

1. Ignore the people who are picking on you. They probably don't believe the rumors. They're just doing it because it makes you mad.

B.S.

2. Why don't you have your father come to school? He should tell them that he's no dope pusher. He's no hippie. He's a dentist. Maybe then the other kids would stop teasing you.
P.E., Fairfax, SC

3. I'm glad to hear that in your town people are embarrassed to take drugs. In our town, the kids seem to be proud of it. If you know you're right, don't let rumors ruin your life. The gossip will die down.

K.N., MN

Question

I want to quit school. I have a good job

lined up. I feel that school has no meaning for me. But my parents won't let me quit. Help me convince them I'm right.

F.W., Maywood, NJ

Answers

1. I don't think you should quit school. A lot of my friends said the same thing. They had "good jobs," but they all came back to school. You only have a few years of school left. Maybe you could work at your job after school.

B.T., Galesburg, IL

2. Don't drop out of school. How good is your job? You'll probably want something better later in life. Then where will you be? You can't get a really good job without finishing high school.

W.G., Edenton, NC

Question

A police station is right near our school. If you are off school grounds, the police pick you up. Your name goes on a truancy list. This happens to kids who are late for school, or who leave for appointments, or who are on free periods. The students planned a strike. But the principal said we would all be expelled. What can we do?

L.H.

Answers

1. Ask the principal to set up a system of passes that the police will go along with. If you have a free period or an appointment, you would carry a special slip.

L.L., Beaversville, IL

2. The kids who are concerned about this could get together. You could elect a representative. He or she could talk to the principal and the police chief. You might come to an agreement. It's worth a try, isn't it?

Ellen, Buffalo, NY

Question

I have a problem in school. The teachers pick on me. That's because my sister had a bad reputation in the same school. What should I do?

J.A.M., Strawton, IN

Answers

1. Tell the teachers you are not like your sister. It could be that you are too self-conscious about your sister. Or it could be the teachers. You have to find out.

C.W., St. Paul, MN

2. Work extra hard. Show the teachers that you are not like your sister.

J.F., Detroit, MI

3. I think you should go to your parents. Maybe they can talk to your counselor.

D.B., Campbell, CA

Question

I'm a guy who has a bad problem in school. I'm supposed to repeat 12th grade this year. Should I try to stick it out, or should I drop out?

M.C., San Jose, CA

Answers

1. I'm 17 and I'm in prison. When I was in 10th grade, I had a lot of problems with my teacher, my friends, and my parents. I chose to drop out of school and get a job. Things went along fine, for a while. Then somehow I got into drugs. Then I started stealing. Now I'm in prison. Almost all the inmates here have followed the same steps I took. Think twice about whatever you do. A high school diploma is more valuable than it seems. I would have graduated this year, if I had stayed in school and faced my problems. I should have had a more optimistic viewpoint. You've just got to hang in there.

"Incarcerated"

2. Do not drop out. There were some guys in our school who had to repeat. Nobody laughed at them. If you drop out, you'll have a harder time finding a job. It's only one more year, and it may help you support yourself better. You could wait a few years and go back to school. But a guy in his 20's would stick out more in 12th grade. In my opinion, it's definitely worth repeating.

N.G., Farmington, NH

Question

I am a 16-year-old boy and I'm in love with my teacher. She is 26. How do I convince myself that it won't work? My mother thinks I'm crazy. My teacher thinks it's cute. All I know is, I'm in love.

S.D., Norfolk, VA

Answers

1. First, talk to your guidance counselor at school. This kind of thing is very normal. If necessary, try to switch out of her class. Then start dating girls your own age. Keep your mind off your teacher. Pretend she's married or something.

C.G., Milwaukee, WI

2. Your teacher is probably dating guys her own age. If you say anything, you'll only make a fool of yourself. This isn't love. It's a crush. Grow up.

G.C., Bronx, NY

3. I had the same problem last year. I really thought I was in love with my biology teacher.

Finally, I got to thinking. It wasn't really love. It was strong admiration. I just admired everything about him. So ask yourself: Is it love? Maybe you just really admire her because of the kind of person she is.

M.T., Columbus, OH

Question

I have a problem with homework. If homework is assigned Monday and is due Friday, I wait till Thursday to do it. Then I'm up till midnight. Please give me some advice on how to stop putting things off.

B.B., St. Petersburg, FL

1. You should space your homework out. Do a little bit each day. Then you can do what you want after it is done. Or you can do what you want before you do it. If this doesn't work out, ask your teacher for help. Maybe you both can figure something out.

L.B., Cincinnati, OH

2. Man, you ought to stop putting things off until the last minute. Suppose you had a chance to get the prettiest girl in town. Would you put it off? No way! Well, you shouldn't put off homework, either. If you put off homework, no education. No education, no job. No job, no money. No money, no girls. No girls, no nothing! So get busy.

D.H., Tampa, FL

3. I used to have this same problem. Then, once I had to miss an important opportunity because I was knee-deep in homework. So I overcame the problem. If you do your homework in small doses, it won't seem so bad.

L.P., Sharptown, MD

Question

We have two ball fields at our school. One is for softball. The other is for hardball. They won't let girls play hardball, because they say it is a boys' game. Also, the boys have a basketball team. But the girls don't. Girls *do* like sports. And they can play them as well as boys. But how can I convince the teachers that this is true?

Female Sports Player

Answers

1. I think you are right. If girls want to play hardball, they should be able to. This year our school let boys try out for cheerleading. (None did.) But girls can't try out for the basketball team.

B.E.

2. When we want something reasonable at our school, we write a petition. We get people to sign it. Then we take it to the principal. If it is within reason, he agrees to it.

C.E., St. Augustine, FL

3. Talk to a female teacher. She might have

been in the same situation. Tell her you should
have a chance to prove that girls can play
sports well.

K.C., Brockton, MA

Question

Everyone in my class thinks I'm smart.
I keep telling them that I'm not. What can
I do?

B.M.L., Arnold, MD

Answers

1. Let them keep on calling you smart. It's
a compliment. You should enjoy it.

St. Louis, MO

2. Are you sure that you aren't causing this
trouble yourself? Make sure you aren't some
kind of show-off. It's nice to be smart. But
it's a drag to have someone around who
keeps acting like a smart guy all the time.

J.N., Springfield, MA

Question

When I was in 5th and 6th grades, I got
A's and B's. Now that I'm in high school, I'm
getting C's and D's. I'm trying harder than
I ever did before. How can I get better
grades?

"Help!"

Answers

1. Try watching less TV. Study during the

time you used to spend watching TV. Just watch TV on weekends. I had the same problem. I tried this and it worked for me.

A.E.R., Bronx, NY

2. The work in the 5th and 6th grade may have been easier. Have you tried asking a teacher for extra help? Cheer up. Don't hesitate to ask for help. If you keep trying, your grades will probably improve.

J.F., Vallejo, CA

3. Think about why your grades are so low. Is it because you don't understand the work? Or you don't have enough time to study? Do tests make you so nervous that you fail them? Or does something distract you when you try to work? Don't go to a guidance counselor, if you can help it. He probably doesn't know enough about you and the work you're doing. Ask your teachers for help. Explain to them that you're trying your best but still having trouble. Your teachers might be glad to coach you. Sometimes spending just one half hour with people who know what they're talking about can help. It can make the difference between walking in a fog, or on a cloud.

D.R., Forest Hills, NY

Question

Our problem is about sports. Whenever our class is challenged by another class, the boys take over. They give out the positions and leave the girls out. We've tried to reason with them. But they just ignore us. We're not boy crazy. But we have our rights. What should we do?

Desperate

Answers

1. The next time the boys leave you out, get together with the other girls. Start yelling, "You're no better than we are!" They'll give in if you stand up to them. You've got to stick up for your rights. No one else will do it for you.

B.K., Lenox, MA

2. The boys and girls in my class get along fine. They let us do everything they do because we can do it. Show the boys in your class that you can do the same things.

S.K., Hayward, CA

Question

My class has a problem with our teacher. He doesn't explain things clearly. If you say something, he says he'll see you after school. But sometimes we need help right away. What should we do?

C.P.

Answers

1. I had a teacher like yours. I kind of liked

the subject. But I failed the course because
I couldn't understand the teacher. I think
you should tell the principal.

T.E., Slinger, WI

2. I'd talk with the teacher after school. Tell
him that you would appreciate it if he would
help you. If this doesn't work, go to your
counselor for help.

T.F., West Hartford, CT

Question

I'm always talking back to my teachers. I
don't mean to do it. But it just happens. I
know it annoys the teachers very much.
After I do it, I tell myself it won't happen
again. But the same thing happens again. Do
you have any advice for me?

"Need Help," Brooklyn, NY

Answers

1. Talk to your teachers and your guidance
counselor. Tell them you're trying to stop
talking back. Maybe they can help you break
this habit.

T.S., Columbus, OH

2. Calm down. You may be yelling at your
teachers because you are uptight about
things at home. Take life a little easier.
Maybe you should have a hobby to help you
relax.

M.C., Belleville, NJ

Question

I go to a school where all the students work in one giant room. It's so noisy, I can't think. What can I do?

A.M., Atlanta, GA

Answer

Ask the teachers if they can do something about the noise. Or maybe you could use ear plugs when working on your own.

J.M., Glendale, NY

Question

The students in our school are always fighting because of racial differences. We would like them to get along better with each other. How can we convince them that everyone is equal?

"Concerned Class"

Answers

1. We had the same problem at our school. The principal closed the school for a "cooling off" period. During that time, the school board held meetings. Parents and student leaders went to these meetings. They talked about the problem. Everyone agreed to try to get along better. I think that you should suggest that your school board try this.

"Concerned Student"

2. Be friendly with students of other races. Try to get to know them. Ask some of them to go to the movies with you and your friends. Or ask them to join you for a soda. If you get to be friends with them, you'll be able to talk about your differences.

J.W., Bronx, NY

Appearance

Question

I can't understand how people can be so cruel. My friends all make fun of me because I have a long nose. They call me all kinds of names. How can I get them to stop this?

O.B.F.

Answers

1. I'm sure your friends aren't trying to be cruel. They just enjoy teasing you. Don't let them see that it bothers you. If you become angry, they'll keep it up. If you show good humor, they'll stop.

M.J.M., Fresno, CA

2. Ask your friends why they put you down.

Maybe they don't feel good about themselves. Maybe they need to build themselves up by putting you down. But aren't they really putting themselves down by not respecting your feelings? I suggest you find friends who respect you for yourself.

C.M., Minneapolis, MN

3. I once had the same problem. Then I learned that they do it just to make you mad. So I started ignoring them. It's not easy, but it works.

S.F., Hobbs, NM

4. I think you should drop these so-called friends. There must be better people in your school or neighborhood.

R.G., Brockton, MA

Question

There's this girl that I really like. But I don't know how to tell her. I don't want to goof up. Also, she is taller than I am. Do you think this is important?

Concerned

Answers

1. The height difference doesn't matter at all. I'm a girl, and I went out with a guy who is six inches shorter than I am. This didn't hurt our relationship at all.

L.T., Syosset, NY

2. Don't worry about being shorter than

111

your girlfriend. Be proud of her. And don't put yourself down.

L.H., Sprakers, NY

3. You should tell this girl that you like her. She might not be aware of it. Then you can find out if she digs another dude. This will save a lot of trouble later. If you really care about her, height won't bother you.

R.S., Detroit, MI

Question

A lot of people in school make fun of me because I have a big head. They call me "Squarehead." This is making me so angry that I'm going to hit someone. I don't like to start fights, but what can I do?

D.L., Passaic, NJ

Answers

1. These people are just trying to make you angry. Make up a joke about someone with a square head. When someone insults you, laugh and tell them the joke. If they see that they can't make you angry any more, they will stop bothering you. I know this is a hard thing to do, but try it.

B.O., Harlingen, TX

2. I'm very short, and a lot of people used to make fun of me. It bothered me. But then I decided to ignore them. I just made believe that I couldn't hear them. Soon they all stopped teasing me.

G.O., Barre, VT

Question

I'm 15 years old, but I look about 12. So a lot of guys don't ask me out. How can I look older?

G.S.

Answers

1. Get a new hairstyle. Wear a little bit of make-up. If you always wear jeans, try wearing a dress every so often. Remember to act your age all the time. This should help you catch some guy's eye.

J.M., Martinsville, VA

2. Just be yourself. Find a guy who has the same interests as you have. He'll like you for the way you act, not for the way you look.

B.J., Fort Collins, CO

Question

I'm fat, and I want to lose weight. My doctor won't give me diet pills. Does anyone know how I can lose these extra pounds?

"Desperate," Los Banos, CA

Answers

1. Ask your doctor to make up a diet plan for you. Follow the diet, and don't eat between meals. This should help you lose weight.

"Helpful," Natick, MA

2. Eat foods like lettuce and citrus fruits, which are good for you and nonfattening. When you eat lunch at school, select a salad plate. Exercise twice a day. Bike riding, walking, and gardening are good exercises. Weigh yourself once a week. Remember not to eat fried foods.

H.D., Midland, TX

Question

I want to go out for football and basketball. But I'm only 5′4″. The other kids on the team are taller. Is there something I can do to grow? Should I forget the whole thing?

L.T., Dover, DE

Answers

1. You *should* try out for the teams. If you're strong, you can still be a good football player. If you can jump, you can still play basketball. Did you ever hear of Cal Murphy? He's short, and he plays pro ball.

V.L., Chicago, IL

2. I tried out for football. I didn't make it.

They said I was too small. This made me very mad. So I set out to show them. I worked hard. Then I tried out the next year. I made first string! You just need faith in yourself. By the way, I am only 5'2".

D.B.

3. I'm a girl, and I'm one of the best football players in the neighborhood. Believe me, I had to work to get the boys to accept me on their teams. Don't let anyone stop you from what you think you can do.

M.D., Beaufort, SC

Question

I have a problem. I am fat, but not too bad looking. The kids call me names because I am fat. Also, because of my weight, I can't do all the things other kids can do. It's so hard to go on a diet. What should I do?

Depressed, Dayton, OH

Answers

1. Go to a doctor. Find out exactly how much weight you should lose. He'll tell you the best way to go about it. Eat well-balanced meals, and don't give up. You *will* lose weight.

T.C., Ferrisburg, VT

2. Try to get more exercise, and go on a diet. Push yourself away from the table. Don't

nibble between meals. This worked for me. I know you can do it, too.

M.B., Dublin, CA

3. I had the same problem, and I decided to do something about it. Before every meal, I would drink one or two glasses of water. Then I would eat only half of what I used to eat. It sure helped. I lost 35 pounds. I hope you try this.

H.A., Kansas City, MO

Question

I can't seem to stop picking at my face when it breaks out. My mother has begged me to stop doing this. Does anyone have a solution?

"Desperate"

Answers

1. I was a face picker, too. I stopped when my friends told me how much it bothered them to see me do this. I was so embarrassed by what they said that I haven't done it since. Just think about how picking at your face must look to other people. That should make you stop.

"Reformed"

2. I had the same problem. I solved it by keeping my hands busy. I knitted. I painted.

I would even call people on the phone just to keep busy.

Talk to your doctor. He can give you special soap or medicine to help your skin heal. Put your hair up at night. Then the oil on your hair won't get on your face when you sleep.

C.H., Platt, NY

Question

I am a boy. I am very clumsy. I bump into things a lot. Someone told me that there are exercises and things you can do to make yourself more coordinated. Does anybody know anything that might help me?

K.L., Chicago, IL

Answers

1. I've seen many people bump into things. Even football players bump into the field goals. I think you should watch yourself and exercise. Take a run every day. Practice walking between things at home. Also, have an eye doctor check your eyes. Don't worry. You may just be going through an awkward stage. You'll probably change when you grow more.

J.D., Haines City, FL

2. I have a suggestion. I am a girl and nearsighted. Before I got my glasses, I was al-

ways bumping into things. Maybe you need glasses, too.

C.C.C., Berkshire, NY

Question

I feel out of place in phys. ed. class. I wasn't allowed to take it for two years because I was sick. Now it seems that everyone else plays better than I do.

I'd really like to try out for a team, but I'm afraid I won't make it. What can I do to become a better athlete?

S.S., Rio Linda, CA

Answers

1. Try out for the team. You might make it. If you don't, at least you'll know you tried. It's better than wondering if you could have made it.

T.J., Cumberland, MD

2. Were you a good athlete before you got sick? Maybe all you need is practice. If you don't improve in sports, remember that not everyone is great at everything. There may be other things that you are good at.

A.G., Framingham, MA

Question

Sometimes I think I must be the weakest

boy in my class. I eat a lot of good food, but I'm still not strong. What should I do to become stronger?

P.M., San Martin, CA

Answers

1. Exercise twice a day. Do push-ups, sit-ups, and chin-ups. Bike riding is also good exercise.

M.M., Baltimore, MD

2. There is a boy in our class who is very weak. But he is a good mechanic. People don't make fun of him because they know what a good mechanic he is. Get involved in something you do well. Then people will respect you.

D.G.

3. Start lifting light weights. Work up to heavier weights. Play as much baseball and other sports as you can. Get plenty of sleep, and keep eating good food. If you do these things, you'll probably get stronger.

C.R., Baltimore, MD

4. Ask your counselor if your school has any body-building courses. If the school doesn't have any, read some books on body building, or join a gym.

M.B., Miami, FL

Question

My mother bites her nails. When she stops, they grow long and pretty. But she always starts biting them again. I am afraid she will get an infection if she keeps doing this. How can I get her to stop?

M.V., Maspeth, NY

Answer

I stopped biting my nails when I started doing needlepoint. That's because my hands were busy. You might suggest this to your mother. If she doesn't like doing needlepoint, she might try knitting.

"A Friend"

Question

There is a couple in our school who make an awful pair. The boy is very skinny and the girl is very fat. People make fun of them. Should I tell them that they make an awful pair? Or should I let them figure it out?

N.H.

Answers

1. I think people are very stupid for making fun of them. Looks are not everything. Personality should count the most. You shouldn't

try to break up their love just because of a few stupid people.

J.S., *Skokie, IL*

2. Remember the saying: "Beauty is in the eye of the beholder." I think that saying has a lot to do with what is *inside* people. So what if he is skinny and she is fat? That doesn't mean a thing.

C.E., *Annapolis, MD*

3. If people looked at the person and not his or her size, I think they would find better people. Believe me, I go to school with a lot of kids who always notice that I'm fat, but never that I can be a nice person. That's being ignorant. Besides, I can't be nice all the time if nobody treats me nicely some of the time.

R.R., *WI*

Question

My father is very old-fashioned. He doesn't like me to wear shoes or clothes that are in style. I've tried talking to him, but he won't listen. How can I convince him that there's nothing wrong with wearing modern clothes?

K.R., *MA*

Answers

1. Buy one or two things that are in style,

but not *too* modern. Your father may not even notice, if you do this slowly.

E.W., Charlotte, NC

2. Maybe your mother can get your father to change his mind. Meanwhile, you might buy midis or maxis. They're in style, but they *look* old-fashioned. So your father shouldn't object to them.

D.H., Anderson, IN

Feelings

Question

My problem is performing for an audience. I love to sing. I sing very well. But whenever I get in front of an audience, I go to pieces. What can I do?

C.H., Minneapolis, MN

Answers

1. I know how you feel. I have preached a few sermons at church. Do what I do. I just block everything out of my mind, except what I'm saying. Just concentrate on what you are singing. Then you'll put more feeling into the words. And you won't be so scared.

A.M., Blacksburg, VA

2. Get up a group to sing with. You'll feel more at ease that way.

B.B., New York, NY

3. I was once in a talent show. I was afraid of the audience. My parents told me to pretend that someone in the audience was wearing polka-dot underwear. Let me tell you, that was the remedy.

C.H., Endicott, NY

Question

I'm always lying. I lie to my friends and even to my parents. I can't seem to stop doing this. Now my friends and my parents don't trust me. What should I do to stop this?

"Fibber"

Answers

1. Lying is one way to escape reality. Ask yourself why you lie. You may lie because you don't trust other people. You have to convince yourself that if you keep on lying people won't trust *you*.

C.T., Orangeburg, SC

2. I used to lie to my parents. But they checked up on me, and found out I was lying. I learned my lesson then. I started telling the truth and they learned to trust me. You can't get away with a lie.

"Ex-Fibber," Baxter, TN

3. Figure out why you lie. Many people lie because they are afraid of making a bad impression. Try to become more aware of other people's lying. Then you'll realize that you're not the only liar around. Everyone lies once in a while. Make a list of all your good qualities. When you read the list you may see that you have so many good qualities that you don't have to lie about them.

J.A.P., Scranton, SC

Question

I almost lost my life when I got hit by a truck. This may be hard to believe, but the truck driver stopped and told me to cross. Then he hit me and drove off. Since I got out of the hospital, I have been very scared of drivers. Do you think I am wrong not to trust drivers any more? What should I do?

E.L., Stockton, CA

Answers

1. I know quite a few truck drivers. Most are nice people. The one who hit you was different. If you met one mean girl, would you say that all girls are mean? This goes for all kinds of people. It's good to be careful when you cross streets. But you don't have to be afraid of every driver.

L.T., Dayton, OH

2. I was in a car accident once. My head hit the dashboard, and I smashed my upper lip. Ever since, I've been scared to death of riding in a car. Still, I have to do it. But now I wear a seat belt and tell drivers if they are driving too fast.

H.P., Starksboro, VT

Question

I always seem to be forgetting things or losing things. One day, I forgot the key to my locker. The next day, I forgot my coat in the locker room. Another day, I lost two things. How can I stop this?

L.M., Baraboo, WI

Answers

1. Before you leave home or school, stop and make sure you have everything you need. Do this when you are ready to leave each class, too.

T.W., Sugar Grove, OH

2. Get a small notebook, and write down everything you have to take with you. Keep the notebok with you all the time. Look at it every so often. Then you might have better luck remembering where your things are.

J.M., Metamora, IL

Question

I am a girl. Not long ago, a little girl asked

me if I will have to join the Army. She had learned that girls will have to join the Army because of Women's Lib. This is what I told her:

There are some women in this world who don't want to act like men. They want the men to control them. They want to stay home and raise children. Just because some women are weird doesn't mean everyone is. I for one don't want to be a man. I was born a girl, and I want to stay one. How about you?

Concerned

Answers

1. Some women want careers that were once considered for men only. Some men want to do things that were considered women's work. People should be able to do what they wish. Boys should not be taught things like it's bad to enjoy poetry. Girls should not be taught things like it's bad to enjoy sports. Staying home and raising children is a very important job. The Women's Movement is not trying to take away your right to do that. We're trying to build a world where men and women can live as equals. Is this so wrong?

P.H., Jackson, KY

2. Being feminine doesn't mean you have to be a housewife. I'm a girl, and I don't want

to act like a man. But we should be socially and mentally equal to men.

Equally Concerned

3. Women today think they have it bad. Well, about 200 years ago, women didn't have what we have today. For example, they had to make their own soap and candles. I could see complaining back then. But we've got it good now. Why push it?

S.A., OH

4. Women's Libbers aren't weird. What *does* seem strange is why a woman would want a man to control her. I'm a girl, and I want to stay one. But I'm good for something besides staying home all day.

A Woman Libber

5. I think "Concerned" is half right. Some women *do* want men to control them. But a woman who wants the same privileges as a man isn't weird. I want a nice man to marry me. But I don't want him to own me like a slave. I want to be a mother. But I also want a job with the same pay as a man would get.

S.S.

6. If men controlled women, this would not be a free country. If you want to stay home, that's fine. But some women don't want to. Is it your right to tell them what to do? That

is like saying a man must pick cotton because he is black.

Angry, Tullahoma, OK

Question

This problem has been bothering me for a long time. How do you get a bully to "bug off"? He's much bigger than I am. And he won't stop bothering me. What should I do?

D.B., Cupertino, CA

Answers

1. Tell him he is not funny. Most likely, he just wants attention. Tell him that picking on a smaller guy is not very brave. Don't try to get him mad. Just don't pay much attention to him.

B.A., Bakers Corner, IN

2. My advice is to avoid him as much as you can. But when you do see him, stand up to him. Don't back down, or act afraid. That's what bullies like. When they see you are afraid, they pick on you even more. Try not to get yourself beat up. But still, don't run away scared.

T.D., Bowie, MD

Question

I am a 14-year-old girl, and I have a paper route after school. My route starts across the street from school. People think it's strange for a girl to have a paper route. But I don't want to give it up. How can I make people see that my job isn't so strange?

A.D., Bean Blossom, IN

Answers

1. In the past few years, many more women have been working at all kinds of jobs. This includes jobs usually done by men. You have the right to work at what you want. Don't pay any attention to the people who put you down. They are jealous, or their pride is hurt.

C.D., Edenton, NC

2. I think it's a good idea for a girl to have a paper route. She can get money that way to buy clothes, books, etc. You shouldn't care what they say.

J.B., Seneca, IL

3. Explain to these people that a paper route is easier than babysitting. Tell them you'd rather do this than watch somebody's kids.

P.E.S., Bronx, NY

Question

I smoke, although I'm only 14 years old. My parents have told me to stop. I'd like to, but I don't know how. Does anyone have any suggestions on how to stop smoking?

D.S., Macedon, NY

Answers

1. Smoke one cigarette less each day for the next two weeks. Then smoke *two* cigarettes less each day for another two weeks. Keep doing this every two weeks. Meanwhile, don't keep any extra cigarettes in the house. And stay away from friends who smoke.

T.J.K., Van Wert, OH

2. Ask your doctor for advice. The doctor may tell you to use one of the products that help people to stop smoking. These are sold in many drug stores. But *don't* use them before talking with your doctor.

G.A., Udall, KS

Feeling Apart

Question

I am in a state institution. Soon I will be getting out. Sometimes I wonder if I will be able to make it in society. I have come a long way since I was sent here. Still, I am afraid I will make the same mistakes that sent me here. I have talked this over with my case workers and counselors. But how can they understand what it's like? I can't keep myself locked up for the rest of my life for fear of goofing up. Please help me.

Worried, OH

Answers

1. Don't worry. Society will accept you. At least, most people will. Don't be hurt if someone makes fun of you. Some people are just like that. Your case workers and counselors probably care about you more than you think. They can help you.

D.B., Auburndale, MA

2. If you really try to stay out of trouble, you will. Try hanging around with a good group of kids. Don't be afraid of what people say. Just go your own way. Try to get a job. This will keep your mind off your problems.

M.K., Kansas City, KS

3. I am the mother of teenage children. I was divorced, and I am going to marry a man who has been in prison. He knows what you are going through. Have faith in yourself. You have paid for your mistakes. Be careful of the places you go and the people you are with. Keep active, and take pride in your job. You'll make it. My husband-to-be did.

D.D., Levittown, PA

Question

I'm 16. For two years, I've been hooked on heroin. I am sinking fast. Can anyone give me some advice?

"Nameless"

Answers

1. Write to Phoenix House, Public Information Office, 164 West 74th St., New York, NY 10023. They can tell you where you can get help in your area. They have programs which help addicts to help themselves.

Two years is a long time to be hooked. But I think you have the courage to give it up. Believe in yourself, and you'll find the strength you need to win.

J.B., South Hempstead, NY

2. Three years ago, my brother was busted for using heroin. He was in prison for two years, and on parole for one year. Now I think he's clean. At first I wouldn't talk to him because he hurt my parents so much. But I talk to him now that I understand his problems.

Stop using heroin. Don't hurt the people who love you. Stop hurting yourself.

"A Friend"

3. You are brave to have your problem printed in a magazine. So you should be brave enough to go to a hospital or medical

center. People there will help you. Or you might look in the phone book for the number of "Bridges." This is a counseling service in some areas. It helps teenagers with problems.

C.L., Merced, CA

4. I was hooked on heroin. I broke the habit by going "cold turkey." I don't recommend this to you. Find someone to help you. Good luck.

"A Friend"

5. My brother had the same problem. He went to a drug rehabilitation center. Now everything is fine. You can do it, too.

"Your Friend"

6. Talk about your problem with a counselor. Tell your parents about it. They may get very upset when you tell them. Be prepared for that. But get off that stuff now. Soon it might be too late. You can't do it alone, so find some help.

"Anonymous"

7. I know kids who have been hooked — and kicked the habit. I know kids who have died from shooting up. I hope you're not one who will die.

Go to a community center that has a drug rehabilitation center. Stay away from kids who use heroin. Admit that you started

shooting up because you had problems. Then
try to solve these problems, one at a time.

"A Friend"

8. Call a crisis center, a clergyman, a doctor.
They can help you get the kind of help you
need. I'm thinking of you and I believe you
can overcome your problem.

C.S., Columbus, OH

Question

I have a drinking problem. I don't know
what to do about it. Can anyone help?

L.S., Bowie, MD

Answers

1. Don't fool around. Go to your doctor or
health center. I am sure they can help you.

J.M., Galesburg, IL

2. There are many organizations and agen-
cies to help kids with drinking problems.
Check in your local phone book. There may
be a branch of Alcoholics Anonymous or
Alateen. Or call a doctor. He would be able
to tell you where to go.

A Friend, Grand Rapids, MI

3. I am a member of Alcoholics Anonymous.
I have not had a drink or any drugs in nine
months. When I joined AA, I didn't think I
could stop drinking. I had been in a hospital

because of drinking. Now I can say that my body can't take any alcohol.

You are not alone. You may have a disease called alcoholism. It can never be really cured, but it can be stopped. If you keep on drinking, it will only get worse. If you want help, call Alcoholics Anonymous.

S.G., Santa Monica, CA

Question

Whenever I go into a store, I steal little things. So far, I haven't been caught, but I'm afraid that soon I will be. I want to stop doing this. Please tell me how I can stop shoplifting.

"Anonymous"

Answers

1. If you really can't stop shoplifting on your own, talk to your parents about it. If they can't help you, talk to your guidance counselor. Or you might talk to a psychologist or psychiatrist. The fact that you can't stop stealing, even though you want to, shows that you have a psychological problem. A professional would be able to help you.

D.K., Miami, FL

2. I had this problem, but I was caught. My parents were very understanding. They

helped me realize how foolish I was being. Your parents would probably help you if you told them about your problem.

"Reformed"

3. Talk to people who are close to you about your problem. Maybe they'll be able to help you. Meanwhile, don't go into stores alone. Take someone with you. If you feel you are being watched, you probably won't take anything.

M.H.S., Irvington, VA

Question

I am the only boy cheerleader at my school. All the kids tease me about this. How can I get them to stop?

Upset

Answers

1. I'm a boy, 16, and I think if you like cheerleading, you should keep doing it. Cheerleading is very interesting. Why should boys, or anyone, be ruled out of something because they are boys, or girls? Being a boy or a girl doesn't tell us what that person is able to do. People talk about the Equal Rights Amendment and that is good. But if a boy goes out for cheerleading, or becomes a typist, he is looked down on. Some people would think that boy is a sissy. If we are going to accept the Equal Rights Amendment for women, we must have the same respect for men. Women today have construction jobs. These were men's jobs in the past. But if that is the kind of work some women want to do, let them do it. Men don't think it's wrong for women to have these jobs, or for girls to play basketball. But they don't think boys should go out for cheerleading. It's not fair to men. Don't let people bother you. There will be more boy cheerleaders in all schools in the future.

L.F., Mascotte, FL

2. Quit cheerleading. If there was a boy cheerleader at my school, I would make fun of him, too.

A.D., Pensacola, FL

3. We have four boy cheerleaders at our school. I'm a girl cheerleader. We all are glad that the boys are willing to cheer. The boys only cheer for the girls' games. It really makes a person feel good to know they are being supported. Think about who your real friends are. Maybe you should let some of your "so-called" friends read this.

"Trying to be Helpful"

4. I'm a cheerleader (girl) and I think it would be neat to have guy cheerleaders. The reason they could be teasing you is because they weren't picked.

C.H., Wright City, MO

5. I'm a guy and I know how you feel. Just stay on top and don't let it get to you. Don't worry because people tease you. Maybe they're trying to get you off the team, so that they can get on.

D.J., Moberly, MO